PERSPECTIVES OF CONTEMPORARY CULTURAL STUDIES

AN APPRECIATION OF TODAY'S PERFORMANCE, MEDIA AND POPULAR CULTURE

DR. ASHIMANANDA GANGOPADHYAY & ARNAB CHAKRABORTY

This book is dedicated to all the respected teachers, thinkers, researchers and practitioners of culture and cultural studies who truly have been the spiritus inspirationis of us.

Contents

Foreword

This book is primarily a collection of articles on the contemporary issues on cultural studies in theory and praxis. It would has been divided into five chapters containing research papers/ articles on the multidisciplinary aspects of cultural studies in relation to literary, performance and media studies in 21st century, that is, to say the post modern era of revolution in the sphere of Information Technology. The book conceptualizes the emerging aspects of culture and its relevant issues in this new world. It shall also make a comparative study between the different manifestations of culture with relevant instances in a particular time-frame.

To study and develop the focal point and the main objective of the book, we have framed a design to locate and evaluate culture as a lens to reflect a broader perspective in the context of society. To justify this issue we have divided the chapters into several disciplines like popular culture, theatre and performance studies, advertisement and new media culture, the impact of narratology and culture etc.

The main idea behind the choice of this area is to provide a comprehensive research work on today's cultural studies from multidisciplinary backdrop primarily for students, research scholars and teachers whose area of interest is cultural studies and social sciences. We have few books to conceptualize the theories of cultural studies but we don't have enough works to study this interesting field of research from different perspectives along with relevant instances. So, this book will have good reference materials and important data for students and researchers.

The book vividly discusses the new dimensions of cultural studies as an emerging discipline. To begin with the theoretical discussion of the development of cultural studies from Birmingham and Frankfurt Schools it is very important to discuss that as a field of study, it has an emerging context in oriental countries or the former colonies of Europe in their higher academia. Here, we mention the context of South Asian countries that have developed a study of their own apart from the Eurocentric study of culture. This book will also discuss this new paradigm of cultural studies and its importance in higher academia to grow some interest among the students. Besides the conventional approach of the study of humanities and social sciences in universities and colleges, cultural studies have been growing up with a new and larger interest. This book will help to study these new approaches with suitable references.

The chapters of the book excluding the introductory and concluding chapters will contemplate largely on these new dimensions of culture and its multidisciplinary approaches for the academia and research. We think the book will help the students very much to have good reference to relate their syllabus and carry on further research.

Key Features of the Book:

• The book is primarily a collection of articles on the new dimensions of cultural studies as an emerging discipline in higher academia.

• It has written with a close connection to the syllabus of the cultural studies and social sciences of Universities and Colleges so that students and researchers will be interested to get the book and also the libraries will collect the book as a reference to the syllabus of those universities.

• It has a unique chapter on Advertisements (both electronic and print) and the perspectives of culture, consumerism and the new idea of capitalism embedded in these.

• The chapter on Theatre Studies has some key points to conceptualize the convergence of culture through theatrical adaptations with the theories of multiculturalism.

• The discussion of Media will help the students of mass communication and media studies will also help *the students as it is included in the new syllabi of universities.*

• It has also chapters on the cultural manifestations like folk and popular culture with regional backdrops and the concept of myth in emerging cultures.

• All the chapters are divided into sections and sub-sections to discuss the focal points with references to provide a comprehensive understanding for the readers who are primarily students and research scholars of colleges and universities.

Dr. Ashimananda Gangyopadhyay
Arnab Chakraborty

Acknowledgements

This book wouldn't have been possible without the continuous support from our teachers, libraries, archival repositories and persons who helped us immensely to access the resources, to collect and analyse data to make this work possible. We owe an enormous debt of gratitude to the cultural studies practitioners for making their works including the publications, manuscripts etc even in the pandemic situations. We are also immensely grateful to the publishers for making the opportunity to publish this work.

Dr. Ashimananda Gangopadhyay
Arnab Chakraborty

I

Introducing and Situating a Theoretical Framework as an Approach to the Interdisciplinary Context of Popular, Folkloric and Cultural Studies

The discussion of contemporary cultural studies theoretically and of course from its practical perspectives has made a paradigmatic shift from the cultural studies at its very beginning, that is, the late 19th century. One of the basic ideas of cultural studies is to view 'culture. as a lens to reflect a broader perspective, in many contexts, the society at large. From the artistic and aesthetic contexts it portrays the societal realities where human life and practices become vivid that ultimately relate to the broader or umbrella term 'culture'.

Folklore as a cultural manifestation offers a journey far from the madding crowd to the backdrop of a serene and rustic canvas to explore the artistic and aesthetic enthusiasm replete with spontaneity. It banishes the polished urbanity or the urbane sophistication and contemplates on humble and rustic life where the essential passions of the heart find a better soil in which they can attain their maturity, to put it after Wordsworth, the high priest of nature. It frees culture from the urban embellishment and depicts life as it is. For this perspective folklore or folk culture picturises the rustic spontaneity, grown up with a proximity of nature. It also offers a variety of tastes in the manifestation of culture with subtle rustic and regional nuances.

The term 'folklore' was first used by William Thoms' in 1846. Thoms conceptualised 'folk' as European peasants. But the term today has shifted from its 19th century conceptual scenario. Like Thoms, Dundes also used the term for peasants relating to a particular class of people belonging to rural or pastoral areas of Europe. The term 'lore' is suggestive of the cultural practices, heritage and legacy, rituals, beliefs of a particular group or sect of people. From the viewpoint of culture it has now got a an important scenario from the societal structure. Though, folklore emerges and develops from a rural or pastoral landscape, it has a great approach towards the urbanity too, especially in the days of rapid urbanisation and IT revolution.

Let us explore some of the major aspects of folkloric studies of culture and literature developed down the ages.

a. One of the major traditions or characteristic tenets of folk literature and culture is its orality or the oral traditions. From the very beginning folklore emerged from the oral traditions using the the folktales or legends orally passed and popularised from one generation to another. Even the great classical, first and primary epics across the globe truly developed from the oral traditions. It did not provide any structured way to interpret the texts as sometimes the complete, compiled and organised 'text' was not found. The use of riddles or proverbs in oral traditions can also be associated to the folk traditions, later used in literature as a large context.

b. Another important aspect of folkloric study of culture is its representation of myth or mythology at large. Myth is also a folk tradition and interpreted largely in literatures. It derives from the ancient times in both the oriental and occidental traditions. So, for the study and practice of folk culture, myth plays a very important role.

c. Presence of simplicity and spontaneity are found in folk traditions as vibrant and prominent tenets. It portrays a spontaneous manifestation of life as it is free of all sophistication and reflects the reality largely focused as down to earth. The simple diction and expressions free of high embellishment, grandeur and decorum make folk literature and culture close to the mass with a more comprehensive approach.

All these three aspects of folk literature and culture make them accessible easily for a large section of society who can enjoy and relate according to their choices. Thus it becomes popular to a large number of people with ease and interest. But the question is how folkloric traditions make cultural confluences in the hey-day of technological revolution and rapid growth of urbanity.

We can all consider this age as an age of fusion. Here, one culture can easily be associated, assimilated and unified to another and merge to a nice proportion where elements from different cultures are found. On a broader context, a multidisciplinary and multicultural impact can be found. Theoretically process of acculturation can easily be related. When we analyse any cultural production we experience the presence of different cultural manifestations culminating to one entity or integral identity. Thus the process of amalgamation of different cultures into one production makes it comprehensive, new and interesting.

It can be said that folkloric traditions also reflect different cultural manifestations into one production. The context of popular culture becomes relevant where the folk conventions are related to the basic theories of popular culture in a very important way that one makes way for another.

If we conceptualise the basic tenets of popular culture, we can contemplate on the following aspects:

a. Popular culture is accepted and made 'popular' by a large section of society who find the reflection of their own choices in the cultural productions or representations.

b. In the concept of Roland Barthes, the term 'popular' makes it clear that it is understood, associated and enjoyed by the largest group of people through which they can express themselves.

c. From the Frankfurt School of Cultural Studies, Raymond Williams comments on the dimensions of culture, founding the rudimentary context of popular culture merging into the cultural traditions to make new dimensions of culture in the developing society through scientific advancements. Adorno and Horkheimer conceptualises 'culture industry' where 'industry' in the context of culture paves the way to the neo-Marxist schools of philosophy analysing 'culture' as a commodity.

d. Popular culture has a commercial dimension too especially in today's world of mass media and social media. Media plays the pivotal role to circulate a concept with a fingertip.

Popular culture today is largely associated with culture studies. As culture studies analyse culture as a lens to reflect a broader perspective to view the cultural manifestations of a particular community. Popular culture has become an integral part of the cultural practice of the concerned community. Carla Freccero in an essay called "Popular Culture: An Introduction" defines popular culture as

I am using the concept of 'popular' with which cultural studies are largely concerned, to talk about the everyday terrain of people without being sure who the people are, that is, without deciding ahead of time and once and for all who is being referred to by the term 'people'.

It can be said that popular culture is related to cultural studies to a large extent where 'popular' reflects the people whose choices, practices and behaviours are closely related. Truly, popular culture is people's culture.

It is important to justify the key-note of this essay with arguments that can support the key aspect, that is, the confluence of cultures with the artistic and aesthetic presence of popular and folk. Here, we can describe the ideas vividly that we have mentioned earlier relating to the impact and use of mass media in culture. it has already been mentioned that folklore is a spontaneous cultural manifestation of a group of people belonging to far from the din and bustle of busy city life. For a long time it was unexplored since the academicians, enthusiasts and researchers have started to explore. Gradually, breaking the shackles of conventional ideas of folk culture being restricted to the idyllic and remote setting, it started approaching the urban hub and got much enthusiasm and popularity. From its cultural perspectives, folk culture also became an academic discipline of study and research. This process of coming to the mainstream of urbanity, folk culture has made a significant paradigm shift with the tenets of popular culture.

From the theoretical paradigms, it can be seen there is a subtle difference between the basic tenets of popular culture and folk culture. it must be mentioned that folklore does not truly make a synonym of popular culture or vice versa.

Though there are thematic and contextual differences between folk and popular culture regarding their origin and development, but toa large extent they are related together. As we have discussed earlier that folklore has got much popularity today in the urban limelight with the amalgamation of popular culture.

One of the major aspects in the study of popular culture is to analyse and elucidate the process of its gaining popularity with the use of social media and mass media. Modern or to be more specific the post-modern era has witnessed the revolution of information technology. Globalisation has denied the geographical or geo-political barriers and the whole world has become a global village where everything can be accessed within a fingertip. Any information can be shared very easily and can be spread out within seconds. The Netizens are well aware of the much popular term 'viral' today on social media and mass media. This gives way to the hey-day of popular culture.

From the earlier discussions it is clear that popular culture has made a new dimension today which is backed up by the support of mass. They make a cultural product or production popular or enthusiastic. In the same way, it makes the folk popular and enthusiastic among the mass. Undoubtedly folklore has its own potentials to be popular but it must not be denied that popular culture makes it more vivid. Using social media and mass media the cultures of different provinces are celebrated throughout the country. Everybody is informed about any festivals or rituals from anywhere of the world and that becomes a cultural product to be made popular and 'sold' on media. From the view of commercialisation and commodification 'culture' becomes a product. As it is an era of fusion we see the cultural performances are presented with an effect of multicultural manifestations. From the television reality shows to online concerts; from stage performances to the social networking site, everywhere we see the cultural confluences which do not reflect any one cultural practice but show different provincial cultures merged into one performance.

Thus the very word 'culture' does not portray any singular and individual tradition or convention but changes its structural and thematic concerns with the change of time and people's practices. Truly a new dimension of culture has been made with a confluence of different cultural practices and found everywhere. From the commercial context, it becomes popular and prosperous, which is their principal concern. In a nutshell culture today for the sake of popularity and prosperity in view of trade and commerce where the involvement, presence and acceptance of mass is largely concerned.

Another aspect of focal discussion for this essay should contemplate on the relevance of contemporary cultural studies that makes it necessary to include it in the higher academia. As an interdisciplinary field of study and research, cultural studies has become an integral entity embedded within the cradle of literature, linguistic studies, social sciences and performance studies. The principal objective of cultural studies being a lens to theorise, analyse and interpret 'culture' to its very core with the societal elements associated to life and livelihood. From this perspective the movements and theoretical developments of this very contextual study and research from the illustrious Birmingham School, Frankfurt School, Neo-Marxist theories and praxis to the twenty first century latest developments it has enriched and has been enriched much experiencing the vicissitudes of societal scenarios.

౪

Works Cited:

1. Schechner, and Brady. *Performance Studies: An Introduction.* Routledge, 2013.

2. Grossberg, Lawrence, et al. *Cultural Studies.* Routledge, 2016.

3. K., Milestone. *Culture Studies: Theory into Practice.* Sage Publications Ltd, 2020.

4. Oswell, David. *Cultural Theory.* SAGE, 2010.

5. Eagleton, Terry. *Literary Theory: An Introduction.* Blackwell Publishing, 2015.

6. Dundes, Alan. *Folklore*. Routledge, 2005.

7. Bertens, Johannes Willem. *Literary Theory the Basics*. Routledge, 2014.

8. Bennett, Jacquie. *Media Studies*. Longman, 2005.

9. Cuddon, John A., and Rafey Habib. *The Penguin Dictionary of Literary Terms and Literary Theory*. Penguin Books, 2014.

10. Schechner, Richard. *Performance Theory*. Routledge, 2015.

ॐ

ॐ

II

Narratology: Classical to Post classical

Introduction

Before Todorov coined the term Narratology in the 1960s, Narratology had already begun to be explored by critics, scholars like Percy Lubbock (The Craft of Fiction, 1920) and Russian Formalists of the early twentieth century. Its definition, theoretical notions, and fields of applications have gone through a lot of radical changes since the 1970s. This article tries to grasp the evolution of Narratology from classical to Post Classical phases. In order to embark upon it one must endeavour to survey the synchronic and diachronic researches done in Narratology since the 1960s. The classical ideas of Narrativity and Narration of Formalists, Structuralists like Claude Levis-Strauss, Roland Barthes, Gerard Genette have undergone quite remarkable revisions and reformulations even in 80s and 90s. Without being obsessed with any one view of Narratology, first of all it would be rewarding in our effort to trace the development of contemporary Narratological researches across the world during the last fifty years or so.

Narratology: Introduction/ Classical and Structural phase

According to Mieke Bal, 'Narratology is the theory of narratives, narrative texts, images, spectacles, events, cultural artefacts that 'tell a story" (Bal, 1999, p.3). In rather simplistic terms, Narratology studies how the story is narrated or represented as the same story may have different texts, performance, traditions, and cultural representations in formal or informal contexts .This term was an English version of the French term narratologie, coined by Tzvetan Todorov in his Grammaire du Décaméron, 1969. Gradually the distinctions between sjuzhet and fabula proposed by the Russian Formalists like Viktor Shklovsky and Vladimir Propp were supported by the Structuralists like Roland Barthes, Levi-Strauss, Genette, Todorov and Griemas; they expressed their initial views mostly in a journal called **Communications** *in 1960s.*

Narratology has become a serious discourse since the assertions made by Claude Levi-Strauss proposed a theory on myths based on Structuralism and Semiotics in his **Anthropologie structural** *(1958) ; he proposed that myth is a variation of narratives upon a universal theme or structure; in other words, in linguistic* analogy of Saussure's **Course in General Linguistics** (**Cours de linguistique générale** , compilation **by** Charles Bally and Albert Sechehaye based on lectures of Ferdinand de Saussure at the University of Geneva during 1906 and 1911) , myth constitutes a language with a grammar; his proposal unified the study of texts, myth and language , with the concepts of individual 'mythemes' as 'phonemes' in linguistics. This proposal could also be detected in Vladimir Propp's **Morphology of the Folktale** (1928); Levi-Strauss's idea of individual units (mythemes') perhaps originated in his rediscovery of Propp's thirty one narrative elements and seven narrative functions in entire gamut of Russian folktales; naturally this Formalist's approach to find form and orders in diversified narratives finds its parallel in linguistic, semiotic study based on langue and parole, on Structural grounds. As Levi-Strauss suggests some kind of binary oppositions within 'mythemes' , A.J.Greimas also expands his theory of three pairs of **actants or structural units** -a) subject-object b) sender-receiver and c) helper- obstructor ; these again correspond to three pairs of binary opposite narratives-i)desire- aim , ii) communications and iii) support vs hindrance.

Roland Barthes' writings from the beginning of his career to the end of his career show an interesting transformation in terms of his theoretical opinions and application of his narrative and linguistic theories. In his 1977 Interview Barthes confessed that earlier he had postulated a grammar of narrative, or a logic of narrative which he had already claimed in his Introduction to the Structural Analysis of Narratives, *originally published in Communications, 1966 and republished later, that 'no one can produce a narrative without referring himself to an implicit system of unit' (Barthes & Duisit, 1975, pp.237–272). His initial model is explained by Frank Whitehead in* **Roland Barthes' Narratology** *(Whitehead, 1992, pp.41–64) His analogy of narratology with structural linguistics is quite abstract, thinks Whitehead. Barthes proposed three levels of narrative hierarchy: functions, actions and narrations; functions are sub grouped into proper Functions and Indices; later functions are further Subdivided into Cardinal functions or Nuclei and Catalysers (Barthes & Duisit, 1975, pp.237-272). In* **S/ Z (1973)** *Barthes identifies 561 Lexias or narrative fragments which in turn are often interrupted by 93 Divagations, according to Whitehead (1992, pp.41–64). In fact in his Narrative analysis of Balzac's 'Sarrasine' , a short story, Barthes identifies five distinct but arbitrary codes'- 1) Hermeneutic Code (HER) ,2) Semic Code (SEM), 3) Symbolic Code, 4) Code of Actions (ACT) and 5) Cultural specific to reference to science (REF). In* **S/Z (1973)** *Barthes certainly made a radical departure from his earlier perspective; no model could be valid in general for all the narrative texts; he claimed that each text has its own narrative theory. This type of effort by Barthes and Levi-Strauss to codify texts and socio-cultural phenomena was felt to be relevant till the 1960s and 1970s.*

This structural approach in anthropology, cultural studies is nothing but an effort to find a continuity in the narrative history of mankind manifested in different cultural aspects. This continuity could be traced from oral culture to written, literary cultures *across the civilizations. Later Gerard Genette derived much of his theory of '**recit**' and '**histoire**' on the basis of **fabula** (story) and **syuzhet** (plot) of Russian Formalists while discussing Proust in his Narrative Discourse (1980). He penetrates further into the narrative voice and the importance of **narrattee**; he distinguishes among '**heterodiegetic**', '**homodiegetic**' and **autodiegetic** narrative voices (Genette, 1980, pp. 189-194). Genette also makes a distinction between **mimesis** (showing) and **diegesis** (narrating) on the basis of Plato's **Republic**. Yet we know it's very difficult to dissect the speeches directly or indirectly uttered by the narrator. This is related to the perspectives of the narrative voice, which Genette defines as **Focalisation** (Genette, 1980,pp. 189-194).*

Focalisation

*Developed by Gerad Genette, the term **Focalisation** connotes not merely, point of view or perspective, but more exclusively and subtly how the narrative is filtered, intruded, interrupted by the narrator's perspective, identity. Accordingly, the narrator could be in Internal, External or Zero or Omniscient positions. Even Third person narration could be executed through Internal Focalisation. Earlier concepts of First, Second and Third person narration may not sufficiently explain such subtlety of narrative filtration, especially in twentieth century, twenty-first century texts, fictional or poetic. This concept takes us to the matter of identification of the narrator with the characters in the text or narration. **Longinus** in his **On the Sublime** speaks about this subtle and efficient* *identification between the narrator and the character's perspectives much earlier; he further cites examples from **Iliad** where Homer often identifies his own emotional intensity with that of Hector's; this is one of many stylistic devices which contribute towards sublimity.*

New Directions and Domains

*However, as further analysis and interpretation continued, these structural approaches and efforts were gradually felt to be inadequate. Barthes, who initially proposed such an approach, later confessed such inadequacy in his 1977 Interview. Earlier Classical approaches were gradually redefined, re-examined and often new fields were explored. Contemporary Narratological studies could be classified into two directions. One seeks to refine the established notions and theories and redefine the theory itself; other seeks to move beyond the limited literary fields into fresh domains hitherto considered irrelevant to the narratological notions. This second direction is wandering into non-literary, non-verbal fields of discourse still. In terms of approaches it could well be divided into Transmedial or Transgeneric, Cognitive and Diachronic or Comparative narratology. These three approaches are grouped as Post Classical in their Introduction to Current **Trends in Narratology** by Monica Fludernik and Greta Olson (2011) . Still in these three approaches we find two directions - to refine and redefine classical established notions of narratology and to move beyond the established fields in Narratology. These two directions are termed as*

'Frame Abiding' and ***'Frame Shattering'*** *narratologies by Fludernik and Olson.Yet the approaches and directions now converge and diverge often among themselves. This so called 'abiding' and 'shattering' tendencies are not as simple as it appears; if we go through few opinions and claims, both theoretical and practical, we find that there are no such pre-conceived notion or intention to oppose or adhere to the Classical Genettean ideas and distinctions; it is only during the course of discussion that the opposition or adherence take place. For instance, Classical narratological discussions hardly attend to concerns of lyric poetry. Critics like **Eva Muller- Zettlemann think that lyrical genres, by essence of language, consist of Narrativity.***

In fact, in recent narratological views, poetry, particularly Lyric, has raised a certain degree of interest. Lyric poetry has long been kept out of the purview of the narrative genre due, although verse plays of the Elizabethan period have been accepted as one of the narrative ones. As we already have said, Aristotle's Poetics on the verse plays has been the source for discussions on Classical Narratology and the classical narratologists must clarify why it should exclude lyric from its theoretical discourse. In 'Poetry, Narratology, Meta-Cognition' Eva Muller- Zettlemann (Olson, 2011,pp.233,234) challenges such biassed assumptions by Manfred Jahn's 'taxonomic isolation of poetry' (Olson, 2011,p.235) . She defies such Classical approaches with an analysis of Christina Rossetti's 'An End' to argue against the assumed non- sequentiality, 'non-mediation' (Olson, 2011,p. 238) and non- dynamism of lyrics. She shows how 'An End' defies the conventional plot of a love-story and the poem 'focuses on love's peripeteia and denouement and sets in at a stage long after the tales of romantic love have drawn to a close' [12] *(Olson, 2011,p.243). In spirit, it must be accepted that the function of language is the essence of poetry itself. To suggest, imply, through a complex and difficult process of aesthetic understanding is the elemental quality of lyric with its brevity. Eva Muller Zettlemann should have relied more on Stylistics, a branch of linguistics, to bare this essence of lyric and display how rich is the aesthetic understanding of poetry through narratological views. Like lyrics, drama has also long been ignored by Narratological studies and research. Dramatic plot has been out of the purview of narratologists for a long time. Now critics like Brian Richardson have stressed upon the importance of 'unconventional' endings in dramas since Shakespeare, emphasising upon 'the ideological and mimetic violence of open and closed endings' in his 'Endings in Drama and Performance: A Theoretical Model'(Olson, 2011,p.188). He refers to Woolf's 'Modern Fiction' which criticises the lineal, surface reality and conventional mode of narration in Nineteenth century fiction. Virginia Woolf, in her* **'Modern Fiction' and 'Mr. Bennett and Mrs. Brown',** *admires Russian authors like Chekhov and young British writers like Lawrence, Joyce for their fresh and vigorous narrative techniques and endings.*

This kind of fresh view on traditional Generic limitations of Narratology within prose fiction enabled others to explore other fields. Since the development of Chomskyan Deep Structures in Linguistics, Universal Grammar, narratologists in the twenty first century, like David Herman, Manfred Jahn and Monika Fludernik synthesised cognitive narratologies with Stylistics which itself is based upon linguistic and literary notions. This led to what is claimed to be Cognitive poetics- an interdisciplinary study with Narratology and Stylistics.

In Post Classical narratology there has been a tendency to expand upon other nonverbal mediums like painting, sculpturing, music , considering them as a kind of potential narratives; lyric and drama have long been studied from Narratological theories . Yet there has been hardly any serious endeavour to compare narrative poetry in oral and verbal forms. Aristotle, who is considered to be the first Narratologist in his Poetics, based all his ideas upon traditional oral narratives and plays which were available to him possibly in both oral and written forms.

Although Poetics by Aristotle had been the source of Classical narratology, critics have shown their reluctance to include it in the narrative genre; this tendency of Classical narratology has been pointed out by Monika Fluderlink (1996, p 333) . Ansgar Nunning and Roy Summer (2006) in 'The Performative Power of Narrative in Drama: On the Forms and Functions of Dramatic Storytelling in Shakespeare's Plays review this bias against drama and assert the narrative quality of Shakespeare's plays (Olson, 2011,pp. 200-231) . They feel his plays offer 'a rich repertoire of diegetic elements for countering the exclusion of drama from narrative research' (Olson, 2011, p. 206)They refer to the Ghost's narrative in **Hamlet**.

Indeed, many such instances of 'diegetic' elements could be found in plays of different genres at different times.

Tel Aviv and beyond

With this growing interest in diverse genres beyond traditionally held 'narrative' genres, serious efforts have been made by certain institutes like Tel Aviv University and Ohio University. Narratology needed new definition and scope to suit the demands of the time.

The Department of Poetics and Comparative Literature at Tel Aviv University established by Benjamin Hrushovsky in the 1960s had a great impact on Narratology; it inspired the scholars to view Narrative from a communicative and reader's point of view. According to Eyal Segal, the outcome of Tel Aviv conferences in the 1960s and 70s paralleled **S/Z** *(1974),* **The Death of the Author** *(1977) by Roland Barthes,* **Structuralist Poetics** *(1975) by Jonathan Culler (Olson, 2011,p. 298) . Since then Narratology has re-emerged and transformed itself, claims John Pier in his 'French Postclassical Narratology' (Olson, 2011,p. 337), as proposed by David Herman in 1997 by the term Postclassical narratology, it apparently opened up new fields and scope for Narratology; yet Nunning cautioned against considering Narratologies as synonymous with 'narrative studies' and that it should not not be confused with narratological criticisms (Olson, 2011,p.340).*

Reformulations

Yet the earlier reservations of the narratologists about genres, sanctity of Classical ideas of Narrative texts, styles were once gone, and reformulations became easier. For instance, in **Unusual and Unnatural narrative Sequences** *Brian Richardson surveys upon the anti- chronological sjuzhet in Elizabeth Howard's The Long View (1956) Harold Pinter's Betrayal (1987), C.H. Sisson's Christopher Homn (1965); this anti chronological sjuzhet is also traced in the first book of* **Iliad** *as Mieke Bal has already pointed it out. Richardson particular observation lies upon B.S.*

Johnson's *The Unfortunates* (1969) which is largely an experimental work of 25 independent sections; the chapters are claimed to be presented in a random sequence, giving the readers a choice to rearrange the sjuzhet in his / her own way, as it is irrelevant for the 'grieving narrator' (Richardson, 2016,p.168) . His search for such 'unnatural narrative sequences' goes into drama, graphic novel, painting. He finds 'negative sjuzeht'(p.173) in Salman Rushdie's Midnight Children (1981) and in The French Lieutenant's Woman (1969) by John Fowles ; the first one, which won Booker Prize, utilises history and fiction to create magic realism; the second one combines history, fiction or an example of 'historiographic metafiction' ; in both the books , Richardson thinks, earlier presented sjuzeht could be replaced by different ones (Richardson, 2016) ; however all these instances of 'unnatural narrative sequences' could be seen just as a creative utilisation of time and space done by the fiction writers of late twentieth century . However, what Richardson's survey and observation show is a larger orientation of the narrators today towards a radical experimentation with point of views and narrative time in general . Narratologists must define, even to redefine, the Classical structuralist, or Formalist terms of narratological studies and criticism.

That is why perhaps, in **On Narrative Sequence: Classical and Postclassical**' Gerald Prince reverts to the basic question as 'What is narrative?' (Baroni, & Revaz, 2016, p.14), as he feels 'Narrative sequences, in particular, are semantic, nor semiotic in nature' (p.15). Although Prince mainly supports the structuralists and classical definition of narratology in his revised edition of **A Dictionary of Narratology** b as 'the study of narrative as a verbal mode of representation of temporally ordered situations and events' (Prince, 2003, p.66) he seems to be quite aware of the evolution of Narratology from classical to post-classical as he defines it as the study of 'nature, form, and functioning of narrative' (p.66). Likewise, his expansions of certain definitions in this book display the evolution of narratology during 1987 to 2003.

Genette, who is considered to be a Classicist or Structuralist as it has been already claimed, provided three basic theoretical assumptions — a) Voice, b) Tense and c) Mode. He is credited to have removed the confusion regarding first person and third person narratives by proposing Homodiegetic and Heterodiegetic narrative voices. Yet his most significant contribution is the concept of Focalization. It is by far the most controversial too. It is Mieke Bal who reformulates this concept as she defines Focalization as 'the relationship between the 'vision', the agent that sees, and that which is seen' (Bal, 1991,p .144), while referring to the seventh century bass- relief of Arjuna -Penance at Mahaballipuram in Southern India . The problem of defining narrative perspectives as Persons or Point of Views continues with Bal, Chatman, Boris Uspensky, Manfred Jahn. Most of them have based their reformulations of Genettian terminologies on novels like One Hundred Years of Solitude (1967) by Gabriel Garcia Marquez.

In his Coming to Terms (1990) Seymour Chatman endorses the view of Genette that the narrator only *speaks and can't see while proposing new terminology like Slant, and Filter Filming Composition Deice. An effort to divulge into other non-literary genres like films. This effort is also evident, especially after the 1990s. In her Fictions of Authority: Women Writers and Narrative Voice (1992) Susan Lanser veers into the gendered identity of the narrative voice. Her earlier work The Narrative Act: Point of View in Prose Fiction (1981) has been much more complex in terms of her sub-classifications Focalization and proposes three broad categories of Stance, Status and Contact. Hilary Dannenberg and Marie Laure Ryan have extended the scope and range of Narratology into the virtual reality of sports, computer games, AI. In her Narrative as Virtual Reality (2001, 2015) Marie-Laure Ryan proposes two terms– Interactivity and Immersion (p.90), contrasting the interaction between the reader and a text with the reader's immersion into the fictional world of the text.*

David Herman applies cognitive science to narrative logic, distinguishing between micro and macro levels of story in his Story Logic (2002). Ansgar Nunning applies his focus upon British fiction and challenges the notion of 'implied author'. His discussions are based on Reader- reception theory and communicative approach. Monika Fludernik, another German narratologist, proposes a new notion of Free Indirect discourse in her The Fictions of Language and the Languages of Fiction (Fludernik 2003,p. 69,70). She further extends the application of cognitive science in her **Towards a Natural" Narratology** *and posits that, in order to distinguish narrativity, we need to discard the idea of plot and embrace the idea of experientiality* (p 69, 70).

Expansion of Metalepsis

*Such expansion of Classical terms like Metalepsis is possible and more and more visible in recent works of scholars and critics. In her Metalepsis in Ancient Greek Literature, Irene de Jong defies the tendency of recent scholars to imply that 'metalepsis' could be exclusive to Modern and PostModern fictions(Jong, 2009) ; she finds her support in Gennett , Fludernik and Wagner who found instances of Metalepsis as far as in Renaissance texts like Arcadia and in Iliad. While making such claim, she broadens the concept of metalepsis from that of Gennette who defines it as 'any intrusion by the extradiegetic narrator or narratee into the diegetic universe (or by diegetic characters into a metadiegetic universe, etc.) or the inverse' (Genette, 1980, pp.234-235). For Jong it means that the principal distinction between, or hierarchy of, levels has been broken down or violated: the narrator enters ('shares') the universe of the characters or, conversely, a character intrudes into the world of the narrator (Jong, 2009, p.89). She finds or rather classifies ,three types of **metalepsis**; the first one is apostrophe; second one is where characters come out of the text and shares the views of the narrating world; third one refers to the 'blending of narrative voices' (p.99,); fourth one is 'fade-out' (p.106) ; she explains that 'fadeout' refers to the merging of 'the world of the narrated and the world of the narrator at the end of the narratives'(p.106). She provides sufficient examples from* **Iliad**, **Odyssey**, *Hymn to Apollo, Theogony by Hesoid. She affirms that* *the aim of such 'transgression of the boundaries between narrative universes' (p.115) in ancient literature is to enhance the seriousness and authenticity in oral narratives unlike that of the postmodern fictions and literature. Such an approach towards classical and ancient oral literature will be beneficial in the fields of comparative studies in ancient, classical oral narratives, even across cultures and space; she further proves that narratological assumptions are still relevant for ancient oral literatures, at least from the perspective of narrative voice.*

Postclassical Narratology: new orientation

In his Narratologies: New Perspectives on narrative Analysis(1999) , David Herman introduces the term **'postclassical narratology'** *and demands its formal distinction from classical, structural narratology ; in their introduction to* **Postclassical Narratology: Approaches and Analyses** *Jan Alber and Monika Fludernik refer to the assumptions of French Structuralists like Roland Barthes, Claude Bermond, A.J. Griemas, Gerard Genette , Tzvetan Todorov and German structuralist like Franz Karl Stanzel as Classical Narratology ; as Herman claims, Fludernik and Alber assert that 'postclassical narratology introduces elaborations of classical narratology that both consolidate and diversify the basic theoretical core of narratology'* [37]*(Alber & Fludernik,2010,p. 2). However they clarify that Herman uses the term narratology in a broader sense to include 'narrative studies'; postclassical narratologies now claim to* *incorporate psychoanalytic and deconstructive approaches towards other literary genres beyond novel, even nonliterary mediums like cartoon, films, history , biography and music; In a sense Postclassical narratology shows a general orientation towards a transdisciplinary approaches ; thus today we speak of Feminist Narratologists, Post-Colonial Narratologists; for instance , as Alber and Fludernik claim, 'postclassical narratologists centrally address the question of how the narrative text is imbued with colonial or neo-colonial discourse that correlates with the oppression of the native populations….' (Alber & Fludernik,2010, p. 8).*

Indeed, Narratology has come a long way after the publications of The Crafts of Fiction (1921) by Percy Lubbock, Aspects of Novel (1927) by E.M. Forster to the recent twenty first century journals like Poetics Today. From earlier concerns with the domain and definition of Narratology, it has now integrated itself with diverse fields of literature and social science like Rhetoric, gender study, psychoanalysis, cultural theories like Post Colonialism.

Recently critics like Walsh and Fludernick have reviewed the theoretical assumptions on Voice, Implied author earlier suggested by Gennette . As in their introduction to Post Classical Narratology Alber and Fludernick point out how Alan Palmer detects **Intermental** *thought as opposed to individual and* **intramental** *thought; as the subject matter of traditional novels is often collective, social .In fact Narratologists like David Herman show how* *narratological concepts can be applied to allied disciplines in Social science. With this the scope of narratology now widens towards non-fiction works like autobiography, history. Cognitive narratology can well describe how memory plays a crucial role in organising both facts and fictions in real life situations. For narratology, now the boundary between fiction and non- fiction is certainly blurred.*

Journals and Research centres

Today Narratological research is reflected through various journals like Style, Narrative, Poetics Today, Poetica .Style is published by Penn State University Press and is edited now by **John V. Knapp ; Narrative is published by Ohio State University ; it claims to publish 'essays on narrative as a kind of discourse, e.g., narrative vs. lyric; film narrative in relation to verbal narrative' ; it is now edited by James Phelan; Poetics Today is published by Duke University Press and is edited chiefly by Milette Shamir of Tel Aviv University and Irene Tucker of University of California. It aims to publish articles 'concerned with developing systematic approaches to the study of literature '.***They certainly represent the latest research on narratology across the world. There are also few centres which organise research on Narratology:* **CRAL** *(Centre de recherches sur les arts et le langage) in Paris, the Porter Institute for Poetics and Semiotics in Tel Aviv, Ohio State University. In order to find the latest enterprise and research findings on narratology, their websites, publications, and conference outcomes now prove to be influential.*

Conclusion

Since the 1980s a lot of experimentation has been done to widen the range of narratological fields, as part of the Post Classical Narratological tendency. From cartoons, films, paintings it now stretches itself up to lyrics, science, apart from other non-verbal fields. Many doubted the classical assumptions without daring to dismiss them since most of the experimentations are about the application of classical narratological theories on diverse and unexpected genres. Yet it must be noted, the classical assumptions were based on certain limited texts within a limited genre of fiction; The earlier theoretical assumptions may not stand up to/ satisfy the contemporary applications of diverse and extremely different genres like lyric, music, films.

⅋

References and Works Cited:

Alber, J., & Fludernik, M. (2010). *Postclassical Narratology: Approaches and Analyses.* Ohio State University Press,2.

Bal, M. (1999). Narratology: *Introduction to the Theory of Narrative* (2nd ed.). University of Toronto Press.

Barthes, R., & Duisit, L. (1975). An Introduction to the Structural Analysis of Narrative. *New Literary History,* 6(2), 237–272. https://doi.org/10.2307/468419

Baroni, R., & Revaz, F. (2016). *Narrative Sequence in Contemporary Narratology (THEORY INTERPRETATION NARRATIV)* (1st ed.). Ohio State University Press, 14-15.

Fludernik, M. (1996). TOWARDS A 'NATURAL' NARRATOLOGY. *Jlse,* 25(2), 97–
141. https://doi.org/10.1515/jlse.1996.25.2.97

Fludernik, M. (2003). *The fictions of language and the languages of fiction.* Routledge.

Genette, G.(1980). **Narrative Discourse.** Cornel University Press,189-194. Genette, G.(1980). **Narrative Discourse.** Cornel University Press, 234-235.

Jong, I. (2009). Metalepsis in ancient Greek literature. In *Narratology and Interpretation* (pp. 87-116). De Gruyter.

John V. Knapp, Editor. (n.d.). *Style.* Penn State University Press. Retrieved February 15, 2022, from https://www.psupress.org/

Journals/jnls_Style.html

Olson, G. (2011). *Current Trends in Narratology (Narratologia)* (1st ed.). de Gruyter, 3-5.

Narrative. (n.d.). Ohio State University Press. Retrieved February 15, 2022, from https://ohiostatepress.org/Narrative.html

Poetics Today. (n.d.). Duke University Press. Retrieved February 15, 2022, from

https://read.dukeupress.edu/poetics-today

Prince, G.(2003). A Dictionary of Narratology. (Revised ed.), University of Nebraska Press.

Richardson, B. (2016). Unnatural Narrative Theory. *Style*, *50*(4), 385–405.https://doi.org/10.5325/style.50.4.0385

Ryan, M. (2015). *Narrative as Virtual Reality 2: Revisiting Immersion and Interactivity in Literature and Electronic Media (Parallax: Re-Visions of Culture and Society (Paperback))* (Illustrated ed.). Johns Hopkins University Press.

Whitehead, F. (1992). Roland Barthes's Narratology. *The Cambridge Quarterly*, *21*(1), 41–64. http://www.jstor.org/stable/42971737

III

Media and Mass: Connecting People with Popular Culture

To develop the focal aspects of this essay, we need to delve deep into the backdrop of some of the major tenets of media studies and research today that address the larger society and connect the 'mass' with 'media'. The principal objective of this essay is to investigate how media in its different forms and perspectives play a pivotal role in the development of communication. It also fulfils the process of reciprocation between media and mass. In this process of communication and connection how media connects people with popular culture, that should also be theorized. From the very days of propagandist agendas during the world wars to the postmodern days of IT Revolution, the role of media has a larger impact on the socio-economic, socio-political amd socio-cultural significations.

The post world war societal situations have witnessed a new role of media with the development of technology. Usually we divide mass media into two major categories:

1. Print media
2. Electronic media

Truly in the hey-day of consumerism and commodity fetishism, media has a great role to play in the development of a 'market' to grab the attractions of the consumers, in the perspective of media, the viewers or the readers. People have their own opportunity to shift from one culture to another, from one media house to another to 'buy' something that suits their own 'taste'. That opportunity may lead to offer a broad market culture where people are free to choose anything according to their wishes. Popular culture has been backed by mass media prominently. This long after the is true that Vividh Bharati for radio and many F.M channels from the decade of 90s and obviously the footing of television after post- Site phase were responsible to enhance popular culture which is really very much related to today's mass media.

The term popular culture has been coined presumably during the 19th century. Probably Herder used the term first. It is believed that two European nations, Greece and Rome have played a very important role to form and cater popular culture. Long, after the introductory phase in the 19th century, during the 2nd half of twentieth century, to be more specific, after the 2nd world war popular culture has engulfed media and has been gaining much popularity and acclaim since then. It is also to be noted that media has gain popularity gradually with its different wings like internet, television, radio, journals etc with the conventions of popular culture.

media and its manifestations (source: internet)

Mass media, during its development in the post 2nd world war phase influenced upon people's tastes and choices. The change of taste did not start up abruptly. Rather, historians demand, this is the impact of industrial revolution in Europe which bred and nurtured the concept of 'middle class'. With the help of media, popular culturebegan to merge with the integral part of life and society. After globalisation, terms such as mass culture, media culture, piopular culture, image culture, consumer culture etc are jumbled up for mass consumption. In "Popular Culture: A Teaching Object", Tony Bennett told that the concept of popular culture is like a melting pot of confused and contradictory meanings. He also opined that the concept may be virtually 'useless' because the concept has no capability to direct any theoretical enquiry to end up to a certain certain destination.

To discuss the whole concept of popular culture in a nutshell is very difficult. This is the produyct for the choice of the majority of people living in the society. It is an accumulation of every form of entertainment such as radio, television, movie, cyber-culture, film, dance, songs, art, literature etc. in the book 'Cultural Theory and Popular Culture', John Storey six definitions about popular culture. These are as follows-

1. Popular culture is simply a culture which is widely favoured or well- liked by many people.
2. It is the culture which is left over after we have decided what high culture is.
3. Popular culture is mass-culture.
4. Popular culture is the culture that originates from the people.
5. Intellectual and moral leadership of the subordinate people.
6. A matter of debate for the post-modernism.

popular culture and media (source: internet)

In today's world, especially, which is driven by the technological devices with the rapid advancement of IT Revolution, media plays the role to connect people around the world with just a fingertip. As an effect of globalisation, the world has become a global village to be connected virtually. The media houses from all its different aspects try to serve according to the taste of their consumers with the tenets of popular culture.

Apart from the theoretical discussion on media and popular culture from the backdrop of the societal situations, we need to discuss it from the perspective of higher academia. With the rapid growth of today's information technology, media has peeped through the curtains of higher academics, in colleges and universities. Following this new endeavour Media Studies has become a popular and interesting course to the students. The courses of Journalism and mass communication have been popular to the students since the 2nd half of twentieth century. In our contemporary world in the first two decades of twenty first century we have seen a growth of Media Studies as an academic discipline. It is also a kind of umbrella term where different aspects of media have been merged to frame a course- structure to suit the academic pursuit. The result is also very interesting. The students from pan-Indian universities and from abroad have been getting interested in Media Studies as they find a good career in the new media houses patronised by both the government and corporate sectors. Especially in the South Asian Countries the universities are trying to develop the courses on Media as Core Courses and also optional courses to offer some comprehensive syllabi for the learners. It is to be noted *that, Media Studies from its very beginning as an academic discipline in the U.S in 1970s, it was spread throughout the globe with rapidity. Soon it became popular in U.K, Germany, France, Spain, India etc. as an academic discipline it incorporates the study into different sections. Such as*

1. Journalism
2. Mass Communication
3. Communication sciences
4. Media sciences
5. Communication studies etc.

For the context of Indian higher academics UGC (University Grants Commission) has encouraged much for the development of media studies. Following the guidelines for a university course, Anna University became the first Indian university to commence a course of Master of Science in Electronic Media Programmes. They have offered mainly two courses; a

five year and a two year courses on electronic media. Their Department of Media Sciences has been working well since 2002 and made some paradigmatic steps for the development of Media Studies as an academic discipline in India.

Let us move on to some theoretical perspective for the development of the objectives of this article. Matthew Arnold told:

Culture was a pursuit of human perfection and therefore a civilization agent.

The comment was a reaction for industrialisation and urbanisation. To him, 'popular' and 'culture' are juxtaposed termsfor a comprehensive concept because of deep rooted form of 'anarchy' in peoples' cultural practices and consumptions. F. R. Leavis seconded him in this regard. In a nutshell he proposed the idea of a small group of classes who can mould the rest of the world and thus a concept of tiered society came into the surface. Later on, Raymond Williams has suggested three definitions and dimensions of culture. To him, culture iis an artistic activity for the intellectuals who can set a way of life for the people. Structuralists and post-structuralists define culture as signifying practices. But to speak to mobilise the way of life with the form of intellectual, artistic activity- any branch of art and literature are to be considered to the fallen definitions given by Williams. According to him, culture belongs to three different realms:

1. Lived culture
2. Period culture
3. Factors connecting to lived and period culture.

The scholars of the Frankfurt School quite opposed to what Arnold and Leavis opined for 'anarchy' in projecting the definition of culture. Rather they claimed for 'conformity'- a situation which may somewhat 'deceived' the masses. In 1944, Theodore

Adorno and Max Horkheimer coined the term 'Cultural Industry' to define Mass Culture more prominently. They focussed on both cultural homogeneity and predictability in this regard. According to this school of thought, culture is similar to any other commodities which can be produced, distributed and consumed by the society. Even Adorno cited an example of classical music in opposition to jazz to describe cultural industry rather made a differentiation between culture and popular culture in one of his representative essays. Here is a chart to show the possible trabnsformations of culture into mass culture according to Frankfurt School:

Culture--------------------------**Mass Culture**
    Real-------------------------------False
    European----------------------- American
    Multidimensional ------------Mono-dimensional
    Active Consumption---------- Passive Consumption
    Individual Creation------------ Mass Production
    Imagination---------- ----------- Distraction
    Negation-------------------------- Social Context

Here, the following image shows a structure relating to the concept of mass media and popular culture and their interdisciplinary context.

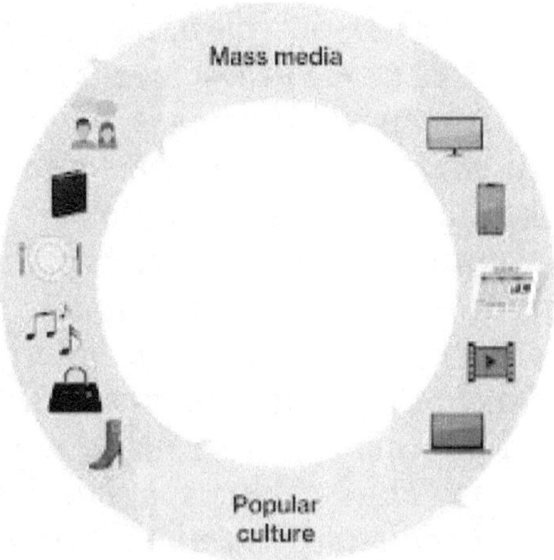

popular culture diagram (source: internet)

To both of them popular culture has a particular orientation to drag the working classes away from the formulation of any revolution by uniting together against capitalism. The scholars of the Frankfurt School did not have much faith on the ethics and morality of the working class people and that's why they feared about their struggle and politics of to be hijacked by the institutions controlled by the capitalistic approach. Although they inclined to the Marxist ideology, most of them allegedly belong to the elite class and that may be another reason for their thought of 'false need' for attaining the fulfillment of materialistic desire instead of being successful in any revolution.

The concept of popular culture is deeply related to mass media and from the perspective of today's culture, none can deny this. Britney Spears is a glaring example of popular culture with the mass media. Her songs were played in various radio stations and she got huge success in making her huge fan-followers with a good number of commercial houses selling the tickets or passes of her concerts among the mass. Mass media including both the electronic and print media like radio, television, tabloid, newspapers, and magazines become helpful partners for spreading popular culture among the mass. Thus there is a band between the local and global scale with symbolic interpretation of spreading culture, popular culture by its name. with the help of technological support , local production can easily cross the special and technological barriers with a strong step towards circulation and transportation among the mass, with more space, with various forms of culture of people.

Stuart Hall suggested about ideology and culture as

Something is left over when one says 'ideology' and something is not present when one says 'culture' (Storey,2001:2)

Storey in his book Cultural Theory and Popular Culture has given five different definitions on ideology. The definitions are given hereunder:

a. Ideology can refer to a systematic body of ideas articulated by a particular group of people.
b. Ideology is used for masking, distortion and concealment.
c. Ideology is used to make ideological forms.
d. Ideology is not a body of ideas, but as a material practice. (Althusser)
e. Ideology is a 'hegemonic' struggle to 'restrict' connotations, to 'fix' particular connotations, to produce new connotations. (Roland Barthes). (Storey, 2001; 3-5)

Let us discuss some of the manifestations of popular culture and its relation to mass media today with the perspectives of social media. It is important to note that in the contemporary world it is the day of internet. With the massive use of internet there's a rapid development of new media or rather the social media like Facebook, Twitter, Whatsapp, My Space etc. which are free spaces for discussion and interaction online. They are somehow serving the purpose of today's coffee house culture on the online mode. This is the easy mode of communication which entangles huge mass as a whole, a mass of different location, different religion, different tastes, castes, creed and cuklture. They pave the ground by allowing 'intellectual curiosity' and also make the platform for 'civic' voices freely participating with their culture by interacting with the whole world. With participating to each other for various and multi-dimensional cultural aspect, people must have the ability to grow tolerance, acceptance by forsaking any stereotyped conception or prejudices.

Moreover, social media largely shares the events of our life. Whether be offline, or online, social media always be the active part of our life. Roughly, there are nine categories for social media:

a. Social networking sites like Facebook, Linkedin, MySpace etc
b. Social news sites like NewsVine, Digg etc
c. Social bookmarking sites like Magnolia, Delicious etc
d. Social sharing sites like Youtube, Flickr etc
e. Social event sites like Meet up
f. Microblogging
g. Wikis like Wikipedia
h. Blogs
a. Forums and message boards.

In the discussion of the perspectives of popular culture and media, to be more specific the the 'social media', it is relevant to discuss the concept of global village in a nutshell. The term was coined by Marshall McLuhan, a media theorist who defended for 'no boundaries, no monopolies of knowledge' for the internet world. In 1980 the report of MacBride Commission under the title 'Many Voices, One World' where he tried to define the problems of communication around the world. In the field of transnational communication, some issues have made a rift between the oriental and the occidental nations. This is true that to the citizens of America, there are so many incidents which are considered as non-issue for them but those may have been sincerely treated as serious issues for other countries or continents. For communication, Western Bloc has some intricacies which have been defined in this report. The unveiling mask of western cultural imperialism or to say 'dominant culture', the dictatorship of the west hadb faced a challenge for the interconnected platform around the world through social media. Straubhaar, La rose and Devenport argued, " An alternative vision of the global future is that media and information technologies will decentralize the global village, so that information and culture will flow in many directions from a variety of sources, with many different messages"(ibid 100). Wilson commented, 'Media presentations in which cultural inputs are drawn from different countries and cultures in this global village.(ibid 101) 'Digital literacy' is also an important phrase while we are talking about the huge users of social media. The matter completely depends upon practicing and handling it properly. Without proper knowledge of the use of social media, one can never optimize one's level of knowledge and span of association. We may cite what greenhow, Robelia and Hughes suggested in this regard, 'Digital literacy includes knowing how and when to use which technologies and knowing which forms and functions are most appropriate for one's purposes". Social media has no territorial jurisdiction of any kind and through it popular culture can be integrated into the academic curriculam. Students with or without exploring their identities, can be a part in some collaborative projects to enhance the value of their education. Such mingling of 'high' and 'low' conventions of education except sticking to any particular hierarchical or traditional approach or such point of view, we can say that the space for sharing experiences in the realm of education may be possible through popular culture.

The concept of Raymond Williams about the perspective of 'culture' can also be discussed in the context of popular culture. There are some more definitions which may tag social media with culture in a broader sense. To Dominick, culture is a "complex concept that refers to the common values, beliefs, social practices, rules and assumptions that bind a group of people together…" People of different attitude, different life-style and different behavior develop their knowledge through inter group communication and thus social media are very much helpful to make each other unknown to known and every culture recognizable with all at the same time.

We have a great deal of instances for popular culture castigated through social media. Basically, the part is evident in linguistic styles and slangs in language. New culture for abbreviation we have got as the beneficiaries of social media such as HBD(Happy Birthday), RIP(Rest in peace), OMG(Oh my God), UWC(you are welcome) etc. and the most interesting interpretation is for LOL because one implies several meaning such as Laugh out loud, Lots of laughter, lots of love etc. there are five types of icons against any post offered by Facebook now- such as like, love, laugh, wow (expressing excellence), sad and anger. Various icons project different sentiments or feelings of people for projecting their opinion and moreover, there are two more options like comment and share which invite the viewers to express elaborately their feelings and point of view against those posts. Now eith these involvements people have two great opportunities:

a.

To make friendship or interact with such people/ community unknown to them. And

b.

They can thrive upon their culture on the wall of social media without any hesitation or fear.

Even so many words have been changed in spelling while they are used in social media or sending messages to somebody else. The list is quite large in size still we would like to mention some of the daily used words such as this, that, is are, you, your, brother, sister, and, congrat6ulations, thanks, great, for, the, birthday, life, love, message etc. The given list shows how such spellings get changed:

This------ Dis

    Congratulations-----------Congrts

    That------------------------Dat

    Thanks----------------------Tnks/ tnqs

    Good------------------------Gud

    Great-----------------------Grt

    Are-------------------------R

    For-------------------------4

    You-------------------------U

    Your------------------------Ur

    Birthday--------------------Bday

    Brother---------------------Bro

    Life------------------------Lyf

    Sister----------------------Sis

    Love------------------------Luv

    and-------------------------Nd/n

message----------------------msg

Thus, a cultural bonding for larger communication has been made up through social media irrespective of belonging to ethnic affinities. Social media users have the habit to give some spaces for their virtual friends to adopt their culture and behavior, ritualistic and religious patterns and of course vice versa.

Here, we must remember that language which originated through signs and symbols and developed gradually through oral culture and practices. With various approaches and behavioral gestures, spoken words were born. Then printed words appeared. But culture should have no language specification: neither written nor spoken or printed form of words. And likewise, popular culture depends on many idiomatic expressions for reaching than that of languages. This is because the world of popular culture is such enriched, different and various that that exchange between communities or groups of people may be free and comfortable in iconic and idiomatic expressions. Different types of slangs, gossips, sending GIFs are examples of such influences of popular culture through social media. In this regard, we may mention a view propounded by Straubhaar, LaRose and Devenport:

" besides languages, other aspects of culture are important in defining audiences: jokes, slangs, historical references, gossip about stars and remarks about current people and events are often culture- and even nation specific. Thus with various expressions, tweets, re-tweets, sharing any post, writing something

on blogs- the interaction and exchange of different culture, popular culture spreads coming out of any clutch of puritan or traditional or mono-dimensional cultural point of view. Rather, a big, wide and open platform has been offered through social media to spread, participate and assume popular culture because all the activities of the users of social media reflect their participation in respect to life, society and reality around. If we consider their behavioral approach and presentation for their approach towards life, parallelly, this platform offers to make attitude for users and of course the reflection of virtual life, somehow, comes down to their real life and vice versa. Thus social media contents and popular culture share a symbiotic relationship to establish each other."

In this respect, we should mention again a comment given by Straubhaar, LaRose and Davenport:

"the ability of social media to define culture may be eroding the power of conventional media. Ever-growing amounts of the news and entertainment are generated by those who do not work for established big media organisations."

The discussion seems unending. Still, we have to conclude. The narrative would like to end up with two comments- one made by John Fiske and another is Dick Hebdige. Hebdiuge in huis Hiding in the Light; On Images and Things told about popular culture,

" What we call popular culture for example, a set of generally available artefacts- films, records, clothes, TV programmes, modes of transport etc- did not emerge in its recognizable contemporary form until the post Second World War period when new consumer products were designed and manufactured for new consumer markets"

John Fiske in his Understanding Popular Culture opined for popular culture to

"the bricolage of uindustrially produced and distributed commodities that must in order to be economically viable and thus to exist at all, offer, a variety of cultural potentialities to a variety of social formations".

This opinion does not quite fit to the previous one with particular regard to market economy , still, the definition focuses upon the social formation which is also an important part for culture. And media are not isolated for framing society or capturing market. It is obvious that media are counterpart of market economy; rather, to say, to mould the new users, to capture the virgin soil, to hold the regular users, media play an important role to prevail over the mind set up of people, public opinion, public demand etc have been formed with media. The type of projection becomes the trend of the day. Advertising also motivates men and women and even children to adopt popular trend of culture. It can be said that popular culture today largely depends on media- social media and mass media both from their own perspective supply huge potentials to establish and sustain popular culture for long across the world.

In the fag-end of our discussion, we can produce some very recent statistics of the usage of social media from some authentic sources. The number of users is increasing with rapidity. It should also be mentioned during the Covid-pandemic days and the horrors and anxiety of lockdown people have chosen and have spent much time on social media and in the same way the number of internet users has increased to the summit. A comprehensive data chart has been attached here as a result of the analysis of the increasing number of social media and internet users.

Newspaper headline during the outbreak of Corona

Source: *https://www.closeup.org/calm-or-chaos-the-role-of-the-media-during-a-crisis/*

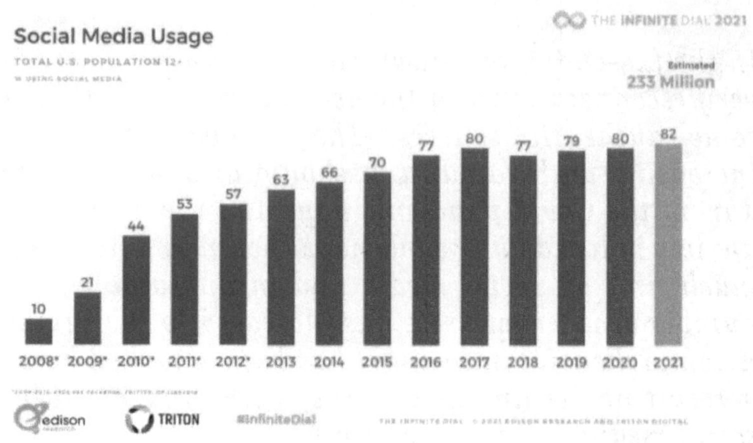

social media usage statistics

https://www.convinceandconvert.com/social-media-research/social-media-usage-statistics/

Bibliography:

1. Storey, John. *Cultural Theory and Popular Culture*: An Introduction, 3rd Ed. 2001. ISBN: 0582423635, Pearson Education Limited, England.
2. Amedie, Jacob. *The Impact of Social Media on Society*, Santa Clara University. https://www.scholarcommons.sce.edu.

3. Crossmen, Ashley. *Social Definition of Popular Culture in Sociology,* https://www.thoughco.com.

4. Ohiagu, O. Pauline, Okorie, Victor. *Social Media: Shaping and Transmitting Popular Culture,* CJOC, Vol 2, No. 1, June 2014, 93-108, https://www.researchgate.net.

5. Parker, HoltN. *Toward a Definition of Popular Culture,* ISSN: 0018-2656, Wesleyan University, History and Theory-50, May-2011, 147-170.

https://onlinelibrary.wiley.com.

1. Valdivia, A.N. *Popular Culture, Encyclopedia of Life Support Systems(EOLSS),* https://www.tazu.ernet.in.

2. Fung, Anthony Y.H Ed. *Asian Popular Culture: The Global (Dis)continuity,* 2013, ISBN: 978-0-415-55717-7, Routledge, New York

3. Gupta, Nilanjana Ed. *Cultural Studies,* 2014, ISBN: 818642399-0, Worldview Publication, New Delhi

4. Pugliatti, Paola. *People and the Popular Cultural and the Culture,* ISSN: 2279-7149, Journal of Early Modern Studies. No. 2. 2013. 19-42, https://www.fupress.com.

• 54 •

IV

Popular Culture, New Media and Advertisements: A Peep into the Consumerist World

Introduction:

The epithet popular culture can be identified with the idea of popuklarity which is the main concern of its theoretical and practical endeavours. In the perspective of the study and critical discussions on cultural studies, popular culture concentrates on the customs or practices, appreciated byb the people who can relate their day to day activities with the arena of a broad cultural manifestation usually and spontaneously performed by the folk. In this aspect, popular culture is often considered as a cultural identity of a large section of society. The study of popular culture in both theory and praxis in the twentieth and twenty first centuries analyzes the multidisciplinary aspect culture and its social perspectives. The socital ambience of popular culture is now reinterpreted as different issues. Those are-

a. Socio- cultural,
b. Socio- political,
c. Socio- economic.

Quite interestingly all these are intimately related to each other. 'Society' as an umbrella term contemplates on different issues of cultural, economic or political scenarios that are well acquainted with a close reading of the perspectives of culture of a particular society.

Background of the study and objectives:

One of the major values of culture is imbedded in its value of arts and aesthetics. Besides, the perspectives of artistic and aesthetic pleasure, different genres of cultural practices in today's world is attributed to its socio economic and and socio-political contexts too. In this perspective, advertisements play a very important role to connect the world of culture and art with mercantile economy and consumerism. In this present article we shall vividly discuss the world of advertisement and its cultural and economic perspectives. We shall try to take up the two genres of advertisements:

a. Electronic advertisement, popularised through electronic media having multi-sensory communicative approach combining audio and visual senses. It includes digital advertising and also mobile advertising through internet which is an important issue today.

b. Print Advertisements or Newspaper or journal advertisement, popularized through print media.

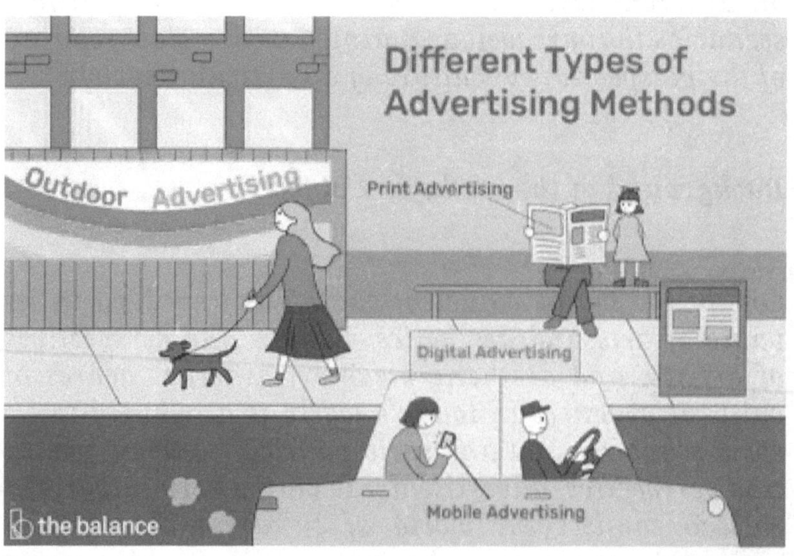

Source: internet

In both the forms, we shall try to negotiate the different objectives of today's advertisements. Such as-

a. Advertisement as a popular form of entertainment
b. Advertisements: connecting media and mass
c. Advertisement and its social perspective
d. Advertisement and cultural scenario
e. Can the advertisements be called a mode of popular culture?
f. Advertisement and the economic world
g. The world of capitalism and consumerism as embedded in the world of advertisement.

It is a globally acknowledged truth that advertisements (both electronic and print) are made from a perspective of art and aesthetics. The art of making advertisements employ men of learning who always try to connect common people to the products in order to attract them to consume the product with their intellectual cultivation of creativity that makes an advertisement attractive and catchy. Therefore we see a galore of talented minds engaging themselves in the world of advertisements.

Thus the art of advertisement does not nourish art for the sake of art only but for the sake of life and society too. The intellectual offspring of the advertisements *amuse the viewers with their creative manifestations. Besides entertainment, advertisements play a pivotal role in connecting media and mass. Media (both electronic and print) with its focal aim to become a medium in creating mass communication, here, connects people and products that must be sold in a consumerist world. The alluring ideas of advertisements enthral people who become convinced with its colourful world of wonder and entertainment. Though media studies have become a popular aspect in the academic scenario of 21st century, it has been a very popular theme in literature for hundreds of years.*

Finding some literary backdrops of advertisements as theme:

Advertisements and its enthralling power to tempt and bemuse the people or consumers has been a popular context of discussion in both literary and non-literary perspectives down the ages. For example, in the world of art and literature(though literature is an inseparable form of art as we can say it the 'literary art' and is not different from the form of art), advertisements and its contexts were developed with the rise of merchant class and mercantile economy during the pre- Renaissance, Renaissance and post-Renaissance days in Europe. In this context 15th, century is important for the rise of merchant class with the fall of agrarian economy. Renaissance has laid the foundations of new trade routes to allure the merchants to traverse and explore the world, ultimately leading to a newer world of trade and commerce. In the literatures of late 15th, 16th and 17th

centuries we have such a reflection of socio- economic world. With the development of trade and commerce, the idea of advertisements too entered interestingly. It was conveyed that the products must be sold and made popular among the buyers. In this context advertisements played a pivotal role in popularizing the products.

We have a plethora of examples from literature. For instance, Ben Jonson's comic and satiric play Volpone (first performed in 1606) has a nice episode thematically intimated with advertisements and its effect on the mass. The famous 'Mountebank Scene' humorously satirizes the temptation of Celia by the advertisement of the product 'Oglio del Scoto' (an ointment to make the women more beautiful hiding their real age and make their youth prolonged) made by Volpone, the central character in disguise of a mountebank or a quack doctor. Celia cannot overcome her passions and the effect of temptation to be more beautiful, although she is the most beautiful woman of the city. She drops her handkerchief from the balcony to buy it. The effect of popular music and other folk elements, cleverly used by Volpone and his companions make a world of temptation to attract the consumers like Celia who gives way to her desires of beauty. Truly, advertisements create the aspect of commodification which is completely adorned by the use of entertaining and alluring devices and popular culture. Here the role of popular culture is to relate people with the product and also the utility of the product using the locale which can be easily accessed by the common people. Thus it becomes so attractive that they become enthusiastic to have the product. Some foreign *products are also sold and made popular through advertisements using the local and popular tastes to meet the expectations of the people. They first make a survey and research to win the favour of consumers very well before launching the product. Thus advertisements incorporate a number of people and a wide range of activities.*

It has been noticed that advertisements have attracted and tempted the common mass from the very beginning. Some more examples can be drawn from literature. We can refer to a very popular and significant poem called Goblin Market, by C.G. Rossetti published in 1869 in the anthology Goblin Market and Other Poems. The poem's setting is a fictitious and strange market in a remote place where the goblins (strange creatures who are neither human beings nor ghosts) sell exotic fruits in the twilight. We see two sisters Lizzie and Laura, the consumers here being attracted to buy the fruits sold by the goblin men. Their repeated cry 'come, buy; come, buy' adds another dimension to their advertisements of the fruits. It tempts Laura very much who cannot refrain from her desires and becomes desperate to buy the fruits. Significantly Laura represents the consumers who always give way to their desires and temptations and spend much in the market. Thus the epithets market, trade, consumerism etc play important role in today's mercantile economy.

The offerings of the goblin-men are very interesting and symbolic here. The poem begins with a picture of the market-place:

"Morning and evening
    Maids heard the goblins' cry
    Come by our orchard fruits,
    Come buy, come buy."

The phrase 'come buy' is taken place twenty times in the poem. Their method of advertisement has an effective power to amuse the customers. The phrases 'all ripe together', 'sweet to tongue' and 'sound to eye' tempt the consumers very much and the way is related and relevant to the present day advertisements. The brainwashing techniques of the advertisements play a great role to trap the consumers as an evil effect of consumerism. One of the greatest of the modern Bengali poets Sankha Ghosh rightly says 'Mukh dheke jaay bigyapaney' ('the face is covered/ hidden by the advertisements').

The exotic fruits in the poem can be interpreted as the metaphors for sexual and material pleasures. Lizzie knows the evil powers of the fruits:

"Their offer should not charm us
    Their evil gifts would harm us.

Like Eve in Milton's Paradise Lost Laura gives way to her temptations and buys the fruits with a 'precious golden lock' of her hair. She has no money to pay for the fruits so she exchanges her beauty to fulfil her desire. This act is symbolic that beauty is commodified by the evil effects of consumerism and in the same way it is also the exploitation of womanhood. One becomes both a consumer and consumed at once like Laura to taste the desires. Laura depicts the madness of desire that must be fulfilled by hook or by crook:

"She sucked and sucked and sucked the more
    Fruits which that unknown orchard bore;
    She sucked until her lips were sore."

These lines have also the undercurrent of sexuality and eroticism. Laura wants some more and determined to quench her thirst of endless passion of sexuality –

"I ate and ate my fill,
    Yet my mouth waters still
    To-morrow night I will
    Buy more."

It is shown that the whole world has become a global market where commercialization has a pivotal role to play. With the aspect of commercialism, consumerism has also entered hand in hand. It peeps through a new idea of capitalism where the capitalist lords invest much in advertisements to sell the products. They use the devices of modern information technology in order to get more and more return. Their use of social media or social networking sites must be negotiated. It clearly indicates to the hey-day of consumerism.

Some instances: the Indian scenario:

Attempts have been made to popularize the advertisements from its very beginning. Lets us discuss some popular Indian television advertisements which are not only popular but also use wit, intellect and wordplay. For instance almost a decade ago there was a popular advertisement of a health-drink called Viva which was shown in different Indian languages, in the Bengali version, we see when a little boy pays respects to his mother through the gesture of 'Pranaam', his mother blesses the boy and the jar of Viva both with a flower and says in Bengali 'Dirghajeevi Hou' which means 'long live', 'succeed' etc. The word Viva itself in English signifies the wish for somebody for his good-luck or his long life. So rhetorically there is a pun on the word Viva which contemplates on the difference of meaning under the similarity of sound. The Bengali word 'Dirghajeevi Hou' also conveys the same meaning simultaneously. Another popular health-drink attracted the consumers with the caption "Taller, Stronger, Sharper", that is, consuming that product would definitely make the students taller, stronger and sharper to their wits according to its advertisement. A regional variation of the same product is found as "Epaang Opaang Jhapaang" which basically don't have any literal or formal meaning but these three words are very popular among people to signify the spontaneity of the children who are not couch-potatoes but very much active in their day-to-day activities like learning, playing etc. it the use of words and popular expressions which makes people to react and to the advertisements. Definitely the use of popular culture and locale helps to build up a market where the business gets developed rapidly.

The presence of popular and illustrious faces also makes the product market-friendly. Today the concept of 'brand-ambassador' can easily be related here. The emerging growth of a 'brand' widely depends on the ambassador who is an illustrious person or what we know as celebrity. It also hikes a huge in the price of the product. And people (to be more precise the 'consumers') always run after or follow the celebrities engaged with the brand.The effect of temptation to by that commodity and to consume ultimately depend on that pretension which is being conveyed by the advertisement engaging a popular face. In real life perhaps or for most of the cases the brand ambassador does not use the brand he is associated with. But this pretension attract the buyers much. Though this idea of 'brand ambassador' is very popular in today's electronic and print advertising but its roots goes almost a century ago. In the popular print advertising or newspaper advertising of 1920s and 30s India we have seen the introduction of popular faces in the brand. for example legendary poet and nobel laureate Rabindranath Tagore had also engaged himself in advertisement published in the then print media. Here we can provide an advertisement of a soap which promoted their business using the praise by Tagore which he has written for them :

"I know of no foreign soaps better than Godrej's and I well make a point of using Godrej's soap"

Godrej's Vegetable Toilet Soap with Tagore's picture and endorsement

Source: internet

In our article this can be a major instance of advertisement where a foreign product tries to make their market in a country using one of the most illustrious faces of that country. Apart from this Tagore was also found to have been engaging himself in advertisements of the products like fountain- pen inks, sweets etc.

We have also found an old advertisement of the car Chevrolet in Bengali. It was published in 1925 in a popular newspaper. The advertisement laid emphasis on the pleasure and comfort it gives as its feature which attracted the aristocrats who could buy this car for 2700 rupees.

for Economical Transportation
CHEVROLET
১৯২৮
১৯২৮
—পূজার সময়—
"সেভরোলে" কার কিনিয়া
আনন্দ উপভোগ করুন!
মূল্য ২৭০০৲
ব্যাটারী ইগ্‌নিসন এবং ব্ল্যাক হুড সহ ম্যাগনেটিক ইগ্‌নিসন ২৫০৲ একষ্ট্রা
অন্যান্য জ্ঞাতব্য বিষয়ের জন্য পত্র লিখুন এবং কিস্তিতে টাকা দিবার কথা জানুন।
অ্যালেনবেরী এণ্ড কোং লিঃ
হেড আপিস এবং কারখানা—৬২ হাজরা রোড, বালিগঞ্জ,—টেলি সাউথ ১২৫
সোরুম ২৪ পার্ক ষ্ট্রীট, কলিকাতা—টেলি কলিকাতা ১৭২৭

Source: internet

In the world of advertisements we have seen a plethora of exponents exhibiting their talents in Indian electronic media. We can mention the illustrious and globally acclaimed filmmaker Satyajit Ray who has also contributed much in advertisements. Another legendary director Rituparno Ghosh is also a renowned name in this context. One cannot forget an advertisement of Borolene, an antiseptic ointment where the tagline goes 'Bango Jibaner ango', that means, 'an inseparable part of the life of Bengal'. It became one of the most popular ones with rapidity. A very interesting aspect of these advertisements is they use the locale or the local taste to attract people always. Quite interestingly when a Hindi television advertisement of a perfume claims Poore India mey to Fogg chaal raaha hain (that means Fogg has become the most popular in India), it tries to dominate the market using the name of the nation. Here, Fogg is the brand which appears in different languages through their advertisements using the public sentiments and taste.

The vibrant presence of regionality makes the advertisements popular and accessible to the people. A very new method used by the agencies is to make different versions of the advertisements for different provinces so that the people get to have a regional and popular taste within the advertisements. Different languages are used to make different versions of these advertisements. A huge number of advertisements use different forms of folk tradition too. For example some sorts of puppetry, scroll painting, forms folk dances, folk music are included as important tools to make the brand popular. As folk culture has been very interesting and popular among people the agencies tactfully use it to make the advertisement widely accessible. The use of folklore and popular culture in advertisements has another important dimension besides the commercial aspect. Often we see the government advertisements use the popular forms of folk culture in their advertisements to create a mass awareness. They perform street theatre, poster painting, scroll painting, puppet theatre, dances like Chhau, Bihu etc to promote the importance of literacy, mass awareness against human trafficking, pollution, dowry system etc. during elections the Election Commission is also found using the forms of folklore in their advertisements to let the people know about the importance of democracy and to let them remind of their electoral roles as electors. These aspects of social awareness are very much embedded in the popular advertisements also. Undoubtedly it has a larger effect on society to engage people in social activities.

The economic world and the aspects of consumerism and commercialization:

With the rapid development of contemporary corporate culture, a huge amount of capital is being transacted in India through advertisements. The multinational companies (MNCs) spend much today for their advertisements and try to incorporate popular faces to reach the mass. Advertisements truly have made a global market using the social media and other manifestations of internet. As internet is widely and very easily accessible to all it strategically targets the internet-world to become popular. A conflict between the print and electronic media in this context can easily palpable. It is the impact of advertisements among the netizens and vice-versa which can be related to the advertisements today.

To relate the economic world with the rapid growth of advertisements it is necessary to point out the aspect of commercialization and the methods taken to reach the global market. To popularize a commodity among the consumers the sellers or agencies use a technique of 4 Ps. Those are:

a. **Product**
b. **Price**
c. **Place**
d. **Promotion**

All these four concepts are related to the idea of commercialization where different measures are taken to popularize the product by attracting the consumers. The chief objective of sellers is to sell their product as soon as possible and make as much as they can from their investments. They invest a huge amount of capital to promote their product in order to get more and more return within a short span of time. Consumers also get entrapped in their eye-catching captions and use of vibrant elements and spontaneity. A new aspect of capitalism silently peeps into our society with this wide range of advertisements. Here we all are consumers who always try to taste the variety of commodities as much as we can often trying to go beyond our capabilities. We cannot resist ourselves from the colourful brands offering mouth-watering products and the 'special discounts' they offer to promote their products.

Source: internet

Here, a very famous poster is provided as a rethinking of Rene Descartes' thought "Cogito ergo sum" which means "I think therefore I am". Here the artist Barbara Kruger made it 'I shop therefore I am'. Though it is has a mocking note but it portrays the real world of today's consumerism.

During the post industrial revolution age, that is, 20th and 21st centuries we have another revolution called the IT Revolution. Truly, information technology has *a larger impact on contemporary economy which has made the world a global village to break all the geographical borders between places. IT goes beyond the borders and reaches all the people through internet. From small scale to larger scale industries, all use electronic media to develop their business. For a relevant perspective, online shopping becomes more popular among the consumers as it saves time and provides the whole market within their fingertips. From the global village we have really been able to see a global bazaar. Thus the idea of commercialization of commodities has a great share with the concept of e-commerce. In every sphere they also make use of advertisements to promote the products.*

Another form of popular electronic advertising takes its shape in the different advertising in radio programmes. Though there is novisual elements to enjoy, the advertising agencies make use of non visual elements like sounds and speeches in their advertisements. They use different forms of musical instruments and voice-overs to promote their business. Everywhere we see the role of advertisements in our day-to-day life as a great impact.

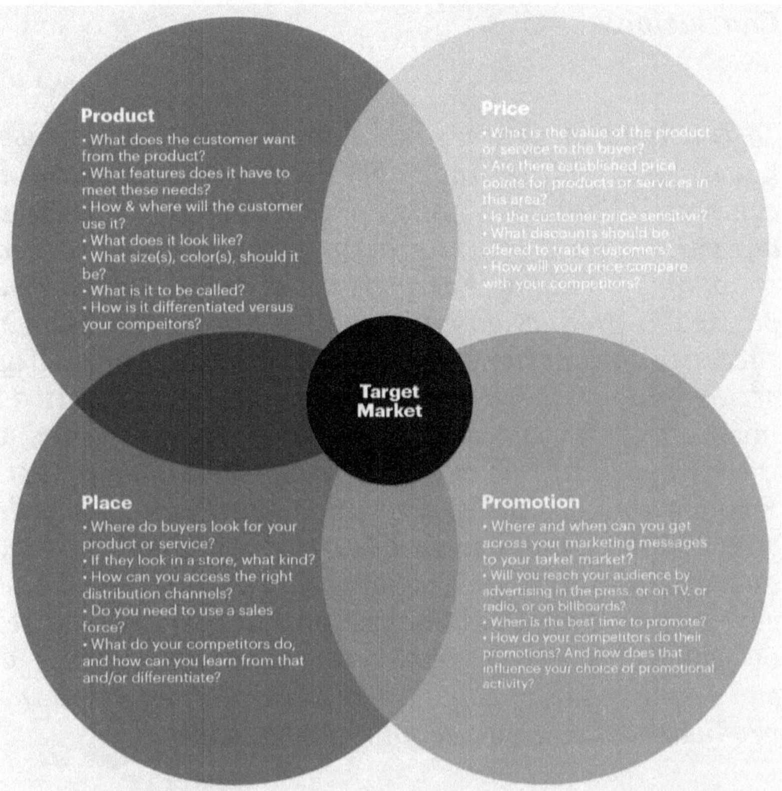

The aspect of commercialization and market oriented economy in ads

Source: internet

Conclusion:

To conclude, it can easily be communicated that we have been witnessing completely a new world commercialization and consumerism where advertising as a medium peeps through every corner of today's economy. Every tit-bit of the business of a particular production, be it small or large depends on a successful promotion. Here, the productivity or utility of the product itself is not given much emphasis as much as it deserve whereas its advertisements has a more important role to play to popularize the product. Brand value is thus a very important concept which goes hand in hand with advertisements. advertising agencies use the golden opportunity to tempt the consumers as the world has become a 'utopia of desire' by the consumer power. Advertisements become a successful mode of popular culture to popularize the products which are to be sold like hot cakes.

৪৩

Works Cited:

Haugen, David M., and Susan Musser. *Popular Culture.* Greenhaven Press, 2011.

VNV, Pickering Michael J. *Popular Culture.* Sage Publ, 2010.

Schechner, Richard, and Sara Brady. *Performance Studies: an Introduction.* Routledge, 2013.

Striff, Erin. *Performance Studies.* Palgrave Macmillan, 2003.

Rossetti, Christina. *Goblin Market and other Poems.* Macmillan, London 1862

Helsinger, Elizabeth K. *Consumer Power and the Utopia of Desire: Christina Rossetti's Goblin Market,*1991

Stafford, Marla R., and Ronald J. Faber. *Advertising, Promotion, and New Media*. M.E. Sharpe, 2005.

Espejo, Roman. *Consumerism*. Greenhaven Press, 2010.

V

Perspectives on Folk and Popular Culture: In search of New Theatrical Adaptations from Western page into Indian Stage

Introduction

Julie Sanders' much celebrated and illustrious book Adaptation and Appropriation (2005) contemplates on the theoretical, artistic, aesthetic and societal dimensions of texts and performances that are adapted and appropriated on the backdrop of a different socio-cultural setting. The author has candidly canvassed the theoretical nuances of adaptation and appropriation with vivid instances. The present article will find out some very recent theatrical adaptations of western texts into Indian context where a plethora of folk elements are used to make a bridge between different cultural perspectives with the study of popular culture. From the perspective of performance studies, folklore and tribal culture become the gateways to envisage a confluence between Orient and Occident. It also signifies the relevance of folk-theatre in the interdisciplinary aspects of literature, folklore, culture studies and performing arts. All these are very much related to the concept of popular culture which relates the day-to-day practices of the mass to that of the artistic and aesthetic aspects of performance. The dialects we practice, the popular rituals or customs found in performances can be identified with the culture represented through the theatrical performances. For example, Shakespeare's A Midsummer Night's Dream becomes 'Fagun Raater Gappo' (Bengali) or Macbeth becomes 'Macbeth Mirror' (Bengali) with different manifestations of folk-performing arts. Similarly, Ibsen's Ghosts is presented as 'Peechha Karti Parchhayyiaan' (Hindi). Folk elements add another dimension to the artistic and aesthetic beauty of performing arts when we see folk musical instruments like 'Madol' and 'Dhamsha' (folk drums) are being played to bemuse the spectators or with the skilful use of folk-arts and crafts. In this way these new adaptations become popular and find new ways of presentation, re-presentation and representation of the rich cultural heritage with the texture of folk and popular culture and the sense of uniqueness.

Background/ Conceptual Framework

One of the major aspects to elucidate the focal aspects of the study, it is necessary to find the interdisciplinary relevance of folk, cultural and performance studies. A definition of folklore can be taken to explain which is structured by Tushar Chattopadhyay in his "Towards a Definition of Folklore"

"Folklore is the total creation of the life practice and ideational pursuit of mainly collective, spontaneous and anonymous effort of an integrated society "

The idea of life practice is spontaneous. It is a vivid and vibrant manifestation of the cultural experiences and existence of a group or community. It is realistic, presenting 'life as it is', banishing the polished urbanity and sophistication. Besides the cultural aspect of folklore, popular culture becomes relevant in the study of performing arts. Popular culture, like folklore, contemplates on the day-to-day life practices of common people which are integral parts of the cultural scenario of a community. In these theatrical performances, the major tenets of popular cultural are largely palpable. As theatre is considered to be one of the most popular genres of performing arts, the relevance of folk elements and the characteristics of popular culture in the perspective of its popularity and enthusiasm must not be denied in it.

It is a vivid idea that the aspects of performing arts and popular culture play a very important role in framing the backdrop of this study. Apart from this idea, the theoretical discussion of performance studies also became an important one to conceptualize this study. Though the primary objective of performance is entertainment but according to the basic thought of Performance Studies states that there are some other aspects too in the course of performance. For instance, Performance Studies view performance as a lens to reflect a greater idea which can reflect the world. Here, Richard Schechner can be considered a pioneer. His book Performance Studies: An Introduction has opened up new thoughts and theoretical endeavour in performance studies and the basic theories of performance. In this book he has made a categorization of different forms of performance. Such as:

a. Artistic Performance and
b. Cultural Performance

For theatrical performances, we can say that it can incorporate artistic performance as it itself is an inseparable part of performing art where different forms of music, dance, storytelling, acting etc mingle together. At the same time theatrical performances reflect a cultural identity of a particular geo-political ambience. It also reflects the cultural identity of a group or sect of people at large.

The Focal points of this Study

In the context of popular culture and folkloric perspectives in these new theatrical productions, the following issues are relevant to frame the main objectives of the study. Those are:

1. To theorize and document the theatrical devices applied to enact the performances.

2. The methods of adaptation and appropriation are to be explored.

3. Over the phase of time it has been found that the theatre practitioners have chosen the source texts from some particular literary and cultural traditions. So it should be analysed the practitioners' exploration and reworking of the source texts.

4. Fernando Ortiz framed the theory of transculturation that has immense social and cultural significance. In the contemporary research on performance studies the theories of performance and transculturation should also be explained.

5. another important objective is to analyze how theatrical traditions are developed with the performances exploring multicultural manifestations and whether the cultural 'blend' is truly possible with this tradition or if it can go beyond the Indianness.

Indian Adaptations of Western Texts: A Cultural Blend from Beginning

An overview of the short history of Indian theatre chronicles legacy of performing or enacting the texts of occident and in the same way adapting or appropriating on the backdrop of Indian society and culture. The first adaptation, according to the critics and historians is M. Jodrell's The Disguise by Gerasim Stepanovich Lebedev, who presented the play as Kalpanik Sambadal in 1795. It also marks the beginning of the journey of Bengali theatre. In the production Golaknath Das, a teacher and practitioner of culture helped Lebedev a lot. Documents have been found to claim that Shakespeare has been much popular in the traditions of enacting occidental plays into Indian languages since 19th century. A very popular Sanskrit production called Vasantika Svapnam by Krishnam Acharya can be taken as a significant instance which has been adapted from Shakespeare's A Midsummer Night's Dream.

If we delve deep into the conceptual framework of the study of literature and its transformation into other generic manifestations like theatrical adaptations, we can find a close relation between literary and cultural studies. In this way literature is enjoyed with the perspective of performance studies. A clear idea of transformation of literature is found. In the same way in the perspective of theatrical adaptation of western texts into Indian contexts an idea of multiculturalism is also detected. Truly it is a cultural blend or cultural confluence. Adaptation thus creates a new text where the instances of both the cultures are palpable.

The context of Folk and Popular Culture: Some Recent Theatrical Productions

To discuss the key-aspect of this paper, I have chosen some recent theatrical adaptations of some English plays which have made a shift from the text to their performances ; from page to the stage giving a new identity and enthusiasm and have added another dimension to the cultural confluence between East and West. Examples are at a galore. Shakespeare has been very much popular through adaptations on Indian stage since 1960s and 70s as discussed earlier. Some recent adaptations are also trying to nourish that legacy and to make the cultural confluence in the first two decades of twentieth century. Among these plays, in this paper I shall discuss three recent productions. These productions / adaptations or appropriations are:

a. **'Macbeth Mirror' (Bengali) from Shakespeare's** *Macbeth*
b. **'Fagun Raater Goppo' (Bengali) from Shakespeare's** ***A Midsummer Night's Dream***
c. **'Romeo and Juliet' (Bengali, English and Hindi) from Shakespeare's** *Romeo and Juliet*
d. **'Doctor Faustus' (Bengali) from Christopher Marlowe's** ***The Tragic History of Doctor Faustus***

To explore 'Macbeth Mirror' first, it is a production by the Kalyani Kalamandalam, a 27 year old Bengali theatre group. The play is directed by Dr. Shantanu Das and the performance-text has been translated from the source text by Prof. Duttatreya Dutt. The play frees Macbeth, the source text from the seventeenth century Scottishand English backdrops. An invocation to Goddess Kali from Hindu myth and scriptures is chanted to serve the prologue. The three witches wearing typical Indian attire and performing the rituals create an ambience of thrill and horror resembling the practices of tantra sadhikas and sadhakas in Indian tradition.

An ambience of folk performances is also created with use and effect of music accompanying instruments like drums like dhaak, dhol, and traditional bells called kasar ghanta. The oil lamps, earthen pots, traditional rituals present and offer a new theatrical experience of Macbeth being performed in a different space.

An important and significant aspect of the performance is the enactment of the whole dramatis personae by three actors on stage. It is a treat of the eyes to experience how they switch over from one character to another. Using the form of folk-theatre, it is a successful improvisation of multi-characterisation in performance. They even don't leave the stage throughout the entire play and don't change the attire. While playing a woman they put on sarees and while enacting a male character they put on girdles red in colour to symbolise the valour and courage of masculinity. Macbeth Mirror also breaks the conventional gap between acts and scenes. The scenes are nicely synchronised here.

'Macbeth Mirror' is a manifestation of a performance with symbolism. The use of hanging ropes from the sky symbolise the knots and hardships of life destined by the fate or nemesis that nobody can escape. Macbeth's entanglement in the knot suggests his hardships and downfall. The use of black colour in the play symbolise darkness, evil and cruelty. Thus the production becomes a unique one to give theatrical adaptations a

new identity by making such a cultural blend where we see the reflections of a mythical magnificence embedded in the term 'mirror' to have a glimpse of the world outside and find out the universality of the human actions and emotions which has no geographical barriers. It has been shown that Macbeth is very much relevant in all ages in the macrocosmic world.

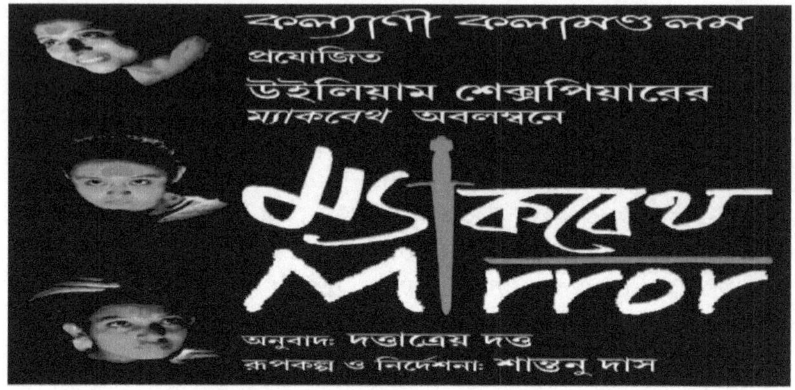

The poster of 'Macbeth Mirror'. Source: internet

A snap of the stage during the performance. Source: internet

Now, let us move on to 'Fagun Raater Goppo', an adaptation of Shakespeare's A Midsummer Night's Dream, which is a production by Rabindra Bharati Theatre Repartoire and directed by Professor Dr. Tarun Pradhan, a renowned theatre practitioner of the contemporary times. Production is based on the translation by Prof Soumitra Basu. Like 'Macbeth Mirror', 'Fagun Raater Goppo' too frees the source text from its particular geographical or demographical locale and becomes an nice appropriation reworked on the Indian scenario. In this production the source text is reworked in the traditions of folk theatre. The rich cultural legacy of Bengali folk theatre is mingled with the major theatrical traditions of India. It is a significant work to enact and represent almost 25 regional elements into one production.

The play begins with elements of one of the oldest traditions of musical popularly known as Jatra or Paala to serve the prologue. The process Of Indianising Shakespeare through folk theatre was indeed difficult. Debesh Chattopadhyay, one of the most renowned theatre persons and a researcher writes in an article in The Times of India (dated 10.12.2016):

"...with its splendid use of folk elements and Shakespearean humour, 'Fagun Raater Goppo' easily stands out as the best Shakespearean production in contemporary times."

Professor Ananda Lal writes in The Telegraph (dated 30.01.2016) -

"...Pradhan's vast expertise in Bengali folk forms enables him to employ a range of performatory modes from Raibeshe to Leto, the Bhanr style of farce and the rhythms of dhamsa and madol, and a set heavily reliant on homegrown rope and bamboo craftsmanship."

In the hey-day of urbanisation and IT revolution when the popular cultural practices are using the tools or devices of post-modern growth with technological advancements, it is tracing theatre to the roots. The environmental consciousness has also been shown with artistic perfection.

A very innovative device has been opted to present the play within the play in comedy significantly. For example the enactment of the group Bharati Opera or the plot of Pyramus and Thisbe being performed in the nuptial ceremony oOf Theseus and Hyppolita must be mentioned. All the characters in 'Fagun Raater Goppo' draw the attentions of the spectators with their excellent performances.

The play also explores the practices of popular culture and the engagement of mass into it. For example the characters are using some popular Bengali and Hindi riddles, slangs, popular songs from movies and jokes. It shows how these engage a lot of people especially in the rural area when they join in some gossips. With the effects of music, dance, mime and folk theatrical elements the play can enthral the audience with vibrant effect of entertainment. The mischievous activities of Puck when he engulfs the forest with mist to deceive the characters nicely suggest the effect of romantic and festive comedies to include disguise, deception and the mistaken identities. The play ends with a message of togetherness as a celebration of life as a triumph of joy and defeat of all disappointments, depression and difficulties. It is truly a rejuvenation and reconciliation of love and laugh.

Finally it can easily be said that 'Fagun Raater Goppo' has created a magical spell on its spectators and has successfully concentrated on the cultural confluence or cultural blend. It must be said that though these productions are adaptations but they are unique in their own way to introduce and incorporate new techniques ultimately contributing a much to the contemporary development of Indian theatre and propagating the sense of uniqueness.

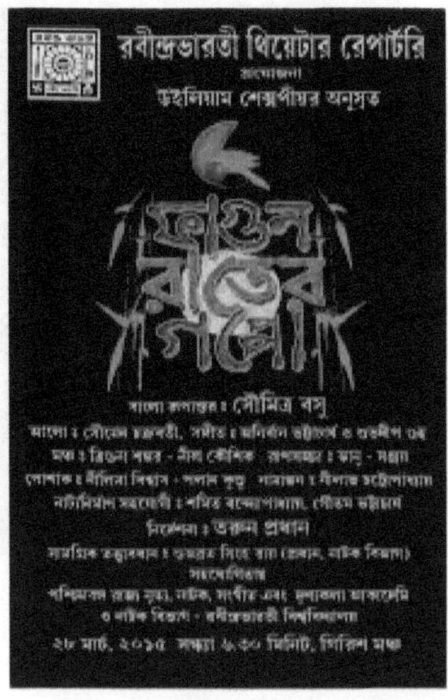

The poster of the production 'Fagun Raater Goppo'.
Source: internet

Oberon and Titania. A snap during the performance.
Source: internet

Another significant and relevant production in this context is 'Romeo and Juliet', an enchanting reworking from Shakespeare's Romeo and Juliet by the group Mukul and Ghetto Tigers, belonging to London. The play is directed by Mukul Ahmed. Here, an almost lost or endangered tradition of two Bengals, West Bengal and Bangladesh has been explored. The tradition is called Paala Gaan- a musical dramatic performance engaging the folk traditions. It resembles the performances of Opera. In rural Bengal and Bangladesh it is a popular form of entertainment as well as traditional cultural practice of the people who have limited access to the cultural practices of urban hubs.

It is a brilliant and courageous work to perform a Shakespearean tragedy into completely different cultural backdrop. It is a multilingual production juxtaposing the languages like Bengali, Hindi, English and Urdu. Different dialects or colloquial terms of Bengali have been nicely merged in the script with other languages. The play begins with an invocation to seek divine inspiration praising the goddess Saraswati, the goddess of learning and culture.

Paala Gaan is performed with the presence of musicians playing various instruments on the stage or space as an element of folk theatre. It performs numerous songs with the accompaniment of music, dance and recitals. A number of folk musical instrumebts are seen to be played on the stage while performing the songs.

A significant dimension is to see the use of Sylheti dialects. Sylhet is a province in Bangladesh. A popular song(Aila re noya daman meaning the gromm comes to marry) has been performed in the wedding of Romeo and Juliet. The groom, according to Sylheti dialect is called 'Daman'. The inclusion of a very popular song into the play is also significant that can engage the audience with joy. The play truly marks its presence to explore new theatrical experiences in appropriating and adapting Shakespeare in such theatrical practices.

It is a magnificent thing to see the cultural blend between East and West. Thus this production becomes much popular and a significant one to make such a cultural confluence using the folk devices in both cultural and performance studies. Apart from the praise it got much criticism too by some eminent scholars and critics for distorting the main essence of a Shakespearean tragedy when they see the play ends with a song celebrating the love with dance presenting a comic manner.

The poster. *Source: internet*

A click in the performance. Source: internet

While the first three productions that we have discussed earlier are from the plays of Shakespeare, the fourth one, i.e, 'Doctor Faustus' owes its source to Christopher Marlowe's Doctor Faustus, a Jacobean play which got much enthusiasm and interest among the audience. The play portrays the tragic downfall of its protagonist Doctor Faustus, a great scholar obtained the doctorate degree from Wittenberg University, Germany. The play is based on the German myth of Faust which Marlowe tactfully uses to develop his plot and characterization. The play depicts Faustus *as a complete Renaissance man in pursuit of knowledge. But at once it is a critique of the practice of knowledge like Necromancy, which is prohibited. Faustus, the protagonist of the play at last suffers a tragic downfall as a result of his agreement or pact, which he has signed with his own blood with the Devils like Lucifer and Mephistophilis for a life full of pleasure for twenty four years. As a result, after the completion of twenty four years, the devils come and take his soul to hell for a cursed life full of eternal suffering. Thematically the play can be called a Morality play which was a popular form of both the play and its theatrical performance during the Medieval Age in the literary history of England.*

The play Doctor Faustus is nicely performed as an adaptation of Marlowe's play by the Kolkata based theatre group called Kasba Arghya with the direction of Manish Mitra, a popular and illustrious theatre director. The group Kasba Arghya is known for their different kind of experimentations and innovations on stage. Here, the production or adaptation keeps the Marlovian theme and structure but shifts from the geographical setting from Germany to India. The protagonist appears on the stage with typical Indian garb like Dhoti. The stage is adorned with popular folk elements and makes a circle inside which the whole play is performed. It also breaks the concept of the proscenium stage and much related to the forms of third theatre. We should better call it a space rather than a stage for it truly banishes the urban sophistication belonging to the concept of stage. The use of folk theatrical forms and musical instruments on stage makes the play more vivid. It is also a fusion of ancient and popular theatre as the play begins with a prologue narrating its main focus. The nice blend of musicality and different dance forms reminds the spectators of different forms of Bengali folk-theatre. This production also portrays the technique of multiple characterization, that is, an actor on the stage plays the roles of different characters. In a nutshell the play also amuses the theatre lovers with its use of various theatrical devices and new experimentations.

A poster of the production. Source: internet

Faustus and Mephistophilis. A click during its performance. *Source: internet*

Another snap from the performance. Source: internet

Apart from these multilingual productions which are mostly from Bengal, we have a plethora of instances from some other provinces of India too which are also to be documented. Undoubtedly Bengal holds a prestigious place in the practice of theatre today. But theatrical practices in India are also popular in Delhi, Maharashtra and Gujarat. With these provinces there is a great development of Hindi, Marathi and Gujarati theatre. Adaptation of the source-texts from the West is also a common practice in these productions. Among those productions we are trying to make a list of the popular ones:

'Ramkali, the Good Woman of Delhi' from Bertolt Brecht's The Good Woman of Shezwan- a production of Darpana Academy of Performing Art and Asmita Theatre Group, directed by Arvind Gaur.

'Teen Paishacha Tamasha' from Brecht's The Threepenny Opera- a Marathi theatrical adaptation directed by P. L Deshpande.

'Ajab Nyaya Vartulacha' from Brecht's Caucasian Chalk Circle is a Marathi adaptation directed by Vijaya Mehta.

Mareechika from Henrik Ibsen's The Lady from the Sea- a Rajasthani adaptation directed by Ila Arun on the backdrop of a popular Rajasthani folk tradition Pabu Ji Ki Phaad. This adaptation is one of the most successful adaptations from Ibsen have been performed several times in India and Norway even in the prestigious International Ibsen Festival and got much acclaim.

'Peer Ghani' from Ibsen's Peer Gynt- a Gujarati adaptation by Ila Arun is another production in this context.

There are more examples from this wide variety of theatrical practices in different provinces of India. It has been shown that adaptation is a very popular method or way to present a theatrical production today where the theatre troups try their hands to rethink the concepts given by the stalwarts in today's context. Behind the choice of the source text, it is generally found that Shakespeare, Ibsen and Brecht have been the most popular playwrights among the groups. Some also have tried their hands with some of the plays by Bernard Shaw. Another important dimension in this regard is that most of the theatre groups use the conventions of popular culture and folk traditions to portray and present their productions. This is how the conventions of popular and folk culture become so relevant in today's theatre (especially urban theatre) where the spectators taste the locale in theatrical productions. The rapid growth of popularity of folk culture among the urban spectators helps to build up a new multicultural manifestation which ultimately develops the cultural legacy of the province or state.

Conclusion:

To conclude, it can be said that these theatrical adaptations or appropriations find new and unexplored dimensions of theatrical performances mixing the global and the local and contributing to the contemporary development of theatrical practice in both page and the stage which has immense social significance. Here, though the source-texts or focal perspectives are borrowed from the West but it concentrates on creating a uniqueness in performance by incorporating new devices into theatre to contextualize the cultural fusion. I think this paper has dwelt on some new areas and arenas of theatrical adaptations incorporating the interdisciplinary approaches to the study of literature, folklore, popular cultural studies and performance where a literary or cultural rejuvenation can be made possible with this cultural blend with the artistic and aesthetic presence of folk culture.

෮෨

Bibliography:

1. Sanders, Julie. *Adaptation and Appropriation. New York :* Routledge, 2015. Print.

2. Hollander, Julia. *Indian Folk Theatres.* London: Routledge, 2007. Print.

3. Gargi, Balwant. *Folk Theatre of India.* South Asia Books, 1992. Print.

4. Laura, Margherita. *Theatre and Adaptation: Return, Rewrite, Repeat.* London : Methuen Drama, 2014. Print.

5. Dutt,Utpal. *On Theatre.* Kolkata : Seagull Books, 2009. Print.

6. Varadpande, M.L. *History of Indian Theatre.* Abhinav Publications, 1987. Print.

7. Shepherd, Simon & Wallis, Mick. *Drama/Theatre/Performance.* New York : Routledge, 2004. Print.

8. Leach, Robert. *Theatre Studies : The Basics.* New York : Routledge, 2008. Print.

9. Chakraborty, Barun Kumar. *Bangiyo Loksanskriti Kosh.* Kolkata: Aparna Book Distributors, 2004. Print.

10. Lal, Ananda & Dasgupta, Chidananda.Ed. *Rasa : The Indian Performing Arts in the Last Twenty-five Years (vol 1) - Theatre and Cinema.* Kolkata : Anamika Kala Sangam Research and Publication, 1995. Print.

11. Chattyopaddhyay, Tushar. *Loksanskritir Tattwarup o Swarup Sandhan.*Kolkata : A. Mukherjee and Company Pvt Ltd, 2002. Print.

12. Chowdhury, Dulal. & Sengupta, Pallab. *Loksanskritir Biswakosh : Encyclopaedia of Folklore of Bengal.* Kolkata : Pustak Bipani, 2013. Print.

13. Sengupta, Goutam. *When the Windows Opened : Communications through Foreign Adaptations on the Bengali Stage.* Global Media Journal - Indian Edition. University of Calcutta. Winter Issue, December 2013.vol 4 no.2

14. Das, Sheelita. *Folk-Theatre : It's Relevance in Development Communication in India.* Global Media Journal –Indian Edition. University of Calcutta. Winter Issue, December 2013.vol 4 no. 2

Prof. (Dr) Ashimananda Gangopadhyay

Prof. (Dr) Ashimananda Gangopadhyay has been teaching as a Professor of Folklore, University of Kalyani, W.B, India. He is a prolific writer and a renowned scholar in the field of Folklore Studies and Popular Culture. In his prestigious teaching career for over 30 years, he has many books and research papers to his credit. He has also given lectures and taught abroad. He has also edited many national and international journals and books and recipient of numerous academic awards. His areas of interest are Cultural Studies, Folklore, Popular Culture, Media Studies etc.

PUBLICATIONS (*Selected list*)

Articles Published in Books

- *Name of the Article –* **"Folklore in the Urban Context and Popular Culture."** *Name of the Book –* **"Folklore in the Urban Context."** Chief Editor – Shamsuzzaman Khan, Publisher – Bangla Academy, Dhaka, Bangladesh; ISBN 984-07-5519-6
- *Name of the Article –* **"Folklore and Media Reflecting Social Change"** *Name of the Book –* **"Social Change And Folklore."** Chief Editor – Shamsuzzaman Khan, Publisher – Bangla Academy, Dhaka, Bangladesh; ISBN 984-07-5641-9
- *Name of the Article –* **"Education through Open-Space Theatre: A Particular case study of 2010 with Audience-Feedback"** *(Co-author). Name of the Book* **"Inclusion and Empowerment Challenges & Opportunities"**. Editor/Chair Professor- Dr. Pranab Kumar Chattopadhyay; Publisher- New Delhi Publisher, New Delhi- 110059, ISBN 978-93-88879-23-1
- *Name of the Article –* **"The Underground: Heaney's Poetic Urbanization of Mythology"** *(Co- author). Name of the Book –* **"Urbanisation and Folklore Emerging Issues and Perspectives."** Editors – Mrinal MEDHI, Pallabi Borah, Mridusmita Mahanta; Publisher – Dept. of Folklore Research, Gauhati University , ISBN

978-93-87035-32-4
- *Name of the Article –* **"Rabindranather Palli Unnayan Bhavnay Palli Shilpa."** *Name of the Book –* **"Rabindranather Palli Unnayan Bhabna"**. Editor – Anjana Saha; Publisher – Sahitya Sangi, ISBN 978- 93-82045-65-6
- *Name of the Articles-*

  - **Gujab**
  - **Gubgubi**
  - **Bichar Gan**
  - **Murshed-er Seba**

  Name of the Book – **"Bangiya Lok Samskriti kosh (Encyclopedia)"**; Editor – Barun Kumar Chakraborti; Publisher – Aparna Book Distributors, ISBN 978-93-81682-09-8

- *Name of the Article –* **"Madhya Juger Kabbyo: Bishoy o Gathon Ritir Boishistyo"**, *Name of the Book –* **"Pragadhunik Bangla Sahitya: Purnanga Mullyayan"** ; Editor – Rejowanul Islam; Publisher – Book Space, ISBN 978-81-922989-0-0
- *Name of the Article –* **"Mahakaler Rather Ghora: Lokojo Upadan"** *Name of the Book –* **"Mahakaler Rather Ghora: Kranti kaler Kathakata;"** Editor – Debobrata Biswas; Publisher – Prajnabikas; ISBN 978-93-81-684-11-5
- *Name of the Article –* **"Hooghly Jelar Prachin Utsav o Melar Khetra SamikkhaKrita Itihas"** *Name of the Book –* **"Itihas Anusandhan"**; Publisher – Paschimbanga Itihas Samsad, ISBN 978-81-910874-3-7
- *Name of the Article –* **"Charai Hassyaros: Ekti Punorbishlesanatwak Patt"** *Name of the Book –* **"Lokosamskriti: Boichitrer Anusandhan;"** Editor – Sumanta Mandal; Publisher – Saha Jatri; ISBN 978- 93-84996-31-4
- *Name of the Article –* **"Loko Galper Ujjwal Jyotishko."** *Name of the book –* **"Parash Tomar;"** Editor – Bijan Kumar Mondal, Publisher – Pustak Bipani, ISBN 978-93-82663-16-4

- *Name of the Article* – **"He Pronomyo Lokocharanik- Laho Pronam"** *Name of the book –*

  "Sraddharghya"; Editors – Jibendu Roy & others, Publisher – Dhrupadi

- *Name of the Article* – **"Chaitanyo uttor Vaishnab Dharmo Sadhonar Itihas: Lokayoto Prekshit"** *Name of the Book –***"Itihas Anushandhan"**, Editor –Manju Chattopadhyay; Publisher – Paschimbanga Itihas Samsad; Kolkata.
- *Name of the Article* – **"Dineshchandra Sen"** *Name of the Book* – **"Bangla Lokosamskriti Charchar Itihas Byaktigato o Pratishthanik Prayash";** Editor –Kakali Dhara Mandal, Publisher – Achin Prakashani; ISBN 978-81-904421-6-9
- *Name of the Articles –*

  - **Bhaba Paglar Gaan**
  - **Bhatiali**
  - **Maij- Bhandarir Gaan**

  Name of the Book – **Bangiyo Loko Sangeet Kosh (Encyclopedia)**, Editor – Barun Kumar Chakraborti; Publisher – Centre for Folklore & Tribal Culture; Ministry of Information & Cultural Dept.; W.B. Govt. Kolkata. ISBN – 978-81-89956-54-7

  Books

- Bangla Probade o Charai Koutuk-Ros o Samaj- Bhabana, Pub.- Grantha Bikash, ISBN 978-98-83018-12-3
- Mymensingh Gitika Porjalochona: Bhinno Bhabnay, Pub.- Grantha Bikash, ISBN 978-93-83018-22-2
- Vaishnab Dhrma o Darshaner Itihas (Pub.- DDE, BU)
- Pragadhunik Bangla Sahitye Loukik- Dharma o Lok-upadan; Pub.- Oityo; Dis - Pustak Bipani

Published Papers in Journals

- *Name of the Paper* – **"Folk Media and Mass Media: A Comparative Analysis in Current Scenario"**

Name of the Journal – **"MEDIA JOURNAL (International Journal of Media)"**; Yr-1, No-2; Editor –
A. Zabir, Publisher(Cont.) – Jatiyo Kabi Kazi Nazrul Islam Viswa Vidyalaya, Bangladesh, ISSN 2414- 2867

- *Name of the Paper* – **"Popular Culture: A Study"** *Name of the Journal* – **"Lokodarpan" (Vol-V)** ;

Editor in Chief Dr. S.K. Mandal, Publisher -Dept. of Folklore, University of Kalyani, ISSN 2454-3683

- *Name of the Paper* – **"Cyber Journalism and India"** *Name of the Journal* – **"MEDIA JOURNAL (International Journal of Media)"**; Yr-1, Vol-1, No-1; Editor – A. Zabir; Publisher (Cont.) – Jatiya Kabi Kazi Nazrul Islam Viswa Vidyalaya, Bangladesh, ISSN 2414-2867
- *Name of the Paper* – **"Communication: Role of Mass Media and Significance of Folklore"**, *Name of the Journal-* **"Lokodarpan" (Vol-IV)** ; Editor- Dr. K. Dhara Mandal, Publisher - Dept. of Folklore, University of Kalyani
- *Name of the Paper* – **"Panchmura - The Terracotta Hub of Bengal: A Contemporary Socio – az Economic Study of Handicraft Workers Engaged In Terracotta Craft"** *Name of the Journal* – **"International Journal of Humanities & Social science Studies" (Vol-V, Issue-III, May- 2019, Page – 42-64),** Publisher – Scholar Publication, Karimganj, Assam, ISSN 2349-6959
- *Name of the Paper* – **"Kabi o Kobiyaler Dondo Bishoyok Samachar"** *Name of the Journal-* **"Lokokobi Bijoy Sarkar Smarak Pattra" (2015);** Editor – Kapil Krishna Thakur, Publisher – Lokokabi Bijoy Sanrkar Smarak Samiti,

- *Name of the Paper –* **"Madhyo Juger Sahityo: Sanjoger Setu,"** *Name of the Journal –* **"Sahitya o Samaskriti"** Editor – Sanjib Kumar Basu, Publisher – Sahityao-o- Samaskrit 10i , Kiran Shankar Roy Rd. Kolkata – 1. R.N. 8869/65
- *Name of the Paper –* **"Ekti Alkaper Sandhane"** *Name of the Journal -* **"Lok o Lokbrittyo;"** Editor – Durgesh Agnihotry; Publisher – Banglar Mukh Prakashan, Kolkata – 700129

- *Name of the Paper -* **"Hooghly Jelar Shoibo Utsab O Mela"** *Name of the Journal –* **'Swadesh Charcha Loke' (Vol – V, Issuse – 9);** Editor – Pranab Sarkar, Published by- Rina Sarkar, Kolkata – 700150

- *Name of the Paper –* **"Mask in Mass Communication: A Particular Case Study with 'Chhanna Chhara Natya Sangha', Adityapur, Birbhum"** *(Co author); Name of the Journal –* **'Vidyamandir Patrika';** Editors – Dr. Arup Kr. Dhabal & others; Published by – Swami Shastra Jnananda, Principal, Ramakrishna Mission Vidyamandira Belur Math, ISSN 23219076

ॐ

Arnab Chakraborty

Arnab Chakraborty is a doctoral research scholar in the Department of English, Raiganj University. He has been teaching English in the Department of English, Srikrishna College, West Bengal as a State Aided College Teacher Category 1 (Govt. Approved). He was previously engaged as a Guest Lecturer in the Department of English, Chakdaha College, West Bengal and Central University of Odisha, Koraput, Odisha. He did his Masters in English from Rabindra Bharati University, Kolkata and Qualified in the National Eligibility Test (UGC-NET). His areas of interest are Theatre and Performance Studies, Cultural Studies and Popular Culture, Victorian Literature and Culture. He has presented papers in the national and international conferences and published research papers and articles in journals and books.

1. Reading Oliver Twist & Goblin Market: Portrayal of Problems & Darkness. **ISBN:978-9380736-88-4** (Published in the book *Reflections of the Growing Mind: Young Adult Literature and Culture*)

2. In Search of Folk Elements: A Study of some Recent Theatrical Adaptations(International Journal of Cultural Studies and Social Sciences) International Peer Reviewed Journal. **ISSN:2347-4777**

3. Victorian Twilight: Women in Society and Women in Literature. **ISBN: 978-81-941702-4-2**(Published in the book*The World of Women: Locality, Nation and Beyond*)

4. Innocence is Killed in Golden Cage: Tagore's The Parrot's Training as a Critique of Education System. ISSN 2277-9809, Online & 2348-9359, Print(*International Research Journal of Management Sociology and Humanities*)

5. Shakespeare in Indian Folk Theatre: Contextualising a Contemporary Theatrical Adaptation of Romeo and Juliet. ISBN 978-81-949267-4-0 (Published in the book *Indian Folklore: Contemplation on Art, Aesthetics and Culture*)

6. Edited a volume entitled Indian Folklore: Contemplation on Art, Aesthetics and Culture. ISBN 978-81-949267-4-0

7. Macbeth Meets Myth Mirrors Mesmerisation published in the book *Macbeth as Macbeth Mirror.* ISBN 978-81-954805-0-0

8. (Re-)reading Hard Times: Dickens's Depiction of Dystopian Disorders published in the journal RAY: International Journal of Multidisciplinary Studies, E-ISSN: 2456-3064 Volume VII, No. 1 / April, 2022